Reflecting on the Past, Shaping the Future

Besides the abundance of natural resources, intellectual property (IP) and technology have played a significant role in Africa's ongoing economic growth and development. Based on these premises, this book reflects on the utilisation of both technology and IP in Africa.

This book brings together expert contributors to examine how Africa can maximise the opportunities afforded by both technology and IP. Drawing from various aspects of life, this book underscores how Africa has failed to use either technology or IP for its development effectively and proposes some reforms. This book explores the intersection of IP and technology in areas such as cultural heritage, tax, education, and agriculture, among others. While the problem of access and adoption underpins the entire book, each chapter offers a different perspective on tackling this issue.

This book will interest researchers and scholars working in the areas of IP, technology law, and development in Africa, as well as lawmakers, policymakers, state actors, and other stakeholders concerned with the access and adoption of technologies in emerging economies. It was originally published as a special issue of the *International Review of Law, Computers & Technology.*

Bukola Faturoti teaches at the School of Law at the University of Hertfordshire, United Kingdom, where he is a member of the Centre for Future Societies Research. His research interests lie in the role of intellectual property and technology in society, especially in the Global South.

Subhajit Basu is Professor of Law and Technology at the University of Leeds, United Kingdom, and is Editor in Chief of *International Review of Law, Computers & Technology.*

Reflecting on the Past, Shaping the Future

Examining Intellectual Property and Technology Law in Africa

Edited by
Bukola Faturoti and Subhajit Basu

Routledge
Taylor & Francis Group
LONDON AND NEW YORK

First published 2025
by Routledge
4 Park Square, Milton Park, Abingdon, Oxon, OX14 4RN

and by Routledge
605 Third Avenue, New York, NY 10158

Routledge is an imprint of the Taylor & Francis Group, an informa business

British Library Cataloguing-in-Publication Data
A catalogue record for this book is available from the British Library

ISBN13: 978-1-032-90819-9 (hbk)
ISBN13: 978-1-032-90820-5 (pbk)
ISBN13: 978-1-003-55994-8 (ebk)

DOI: 10.4324/9781003559948

Typeset in Myriad Pro
by codeMantra

Publisher's Note
The publisher accepts responsibility for any inconsistencies that may have arisen during the conversion of this book from journal articles to book chapters, namely the inclusion of journal terminology.

Contents

Citation Information

The following chapters in this book were originally published in *International Review of Law, Computers & Technology*, volume 36, issue 1 (2022). When citing this material, please use the original page numbering for each article, as follows:

Chapter 1

Protecting intangible cultural heritage in the era of rapid technological advancement
Afolasade A. Adewumi
International Review of Law, Computers & Technology, volume 36, issue 1 (2022), pp. 3–16

Chapter 2

The protection of traditional knowledge under the sui generis regime in Nigeria
Ibijoke P. Byron
International Review of Law, Computers & Technology, volume 36, issue 1 (2022), pp. 17–27

Chapter 3

The digital tax reform for Africa: customised or one-size-fits-all approach?
Nikolai Milogolov and Azamat Berberov
International Review of Law, Computers & Technology, volume 36, issue 1 (2022), pp. 28–47

Chapter 4

Intellectual property rights, agricultural biotechnology and food sufficiency: strengthening the Nigerian intellectual property legal framework for food self-sufficiency in the aftermath of Global Pandemic
Helen Chuma-Okoro and Ifeoma Ann Oluwasemilore
International Review of Law, Computers & Technology, volume 36, issue 1 (2022), pp. 48–67

Chapter 5

Online learning during COVID19 and beyond: a human right based approach to internet access in Africa
Bukola Faturoti
International Review of Law, Computers & Technology, volume 36, issue 1 (2022), pp. 68–90

Notes on Contributors

Afolasade A. Adewumi, Department of Jurisprudence and International Law, Faculty of Law, University of Ibadan, Nigeria.

Subhajit Basu, School of Law, University of Leeds, United Kingdom.

Azamat Berberov, Macroeconomics and Finance Department, Gaidar Institute for Economic Policy, Moscow, Russia; Department of Economic Theory, Financial University under the Government of the Russian Federation, Moscow, Russia.

Ibijoke P. Byron, Department of Private and Property Law, Faculty of Law, University of Ibadan, Nigeria.

Helen Chuma-Okoro, Nigerian Institute of Advanced Legal Studies (NIALS), Lagos, Nigeria.

Bukola Faturoti, School of Law, University of Hertfordshire, United Kingdom.

Nikolai Milogolov, Tax Policy Center, Financial Research Institute under the Ministry of Finance, Moscow, Russia; Laboratory of Tax Policy Research, Russian Presidential Academy of National Economy and Public Administration (RANEPA), Moscow, Russia.

Ifeoma Ann Oluwasemilore, Faculty of Law, University of Lagos, Nigeria.

Introduction – IP and Technology Law in Africa: looking back to look forward

Bukola Faturoti and Subhajit Basu

This collection represents the realisation of our vision to inspire a future of hope, progress, and innovation by gathering scholarship from Africa and about Africa. It showcases the continent's intellectual contributions and its potential to lead in global discourse. Positioned at the intersection of tradition and modernity, this collection explores the transformative role of intellectual property (IP) and technology law in shaping Africa's future, envisioning a path where the continent's rich cultural heritage and emerging technological strengths align to drive equitable and sustainable development.

Until the end of the 1990s, Africa's economic growth was significantly driven by the exploitation of natural resources. However, the early 2000s shifted towards tourism, technology, and a knowledge-based economy. This transition brought attention to the need to protect IP and adopt technology, as many African states experienced unprecedented economic growth. Despite these advances, Africa still lags behind other continents, with its contribution to global innovation remaining marginal. This shortfall has been attributed to weak science and technology capacity, low levels of IP awareness, and limited utilisation of IP due to inadequate legal enforcement. The African Union's Agenda 2063 underscores the importance of science, technology, and innovation in positioning Africa for competitiveness and economic development. However, this aspiration will remain elusive without substantial investment in new technologies and innovation across the agriculture, education, and health sectors. While IP is crucial to realising these scientific, technological, and innovative goals, the Agenda also emphasises the need to strengthen Africa's IP regulatory framework.

Africa's relationship with IP law is deeply rooted in its colonial history. The legal structures inherited by many African nations were primarily designed to serve colonial interests, often at the expense of the cultural and economic realities of indigenous populations. These externally imposed frameworks, which have had a lasting impact, were frequently misaligned with the specific needs of African societies. Even during the negotiations of the Agreement Establishing the World Trade Organization, which included the Agreement on Trade-Related Aspects of Intellectual Property Rights (the TRIPs Agreement), the involvement of African countries was minimal. Consequently, the resulting national IP policies were shaped by a treaty that largely disregarded the national interests of African states.

Beginning with the WIPO Development Agenda 2007, Africa began integrating into the international IP system. This integration's primary objective is to minimise IP costs while maximising its benefits. Many African countries are at the crossroads of initiating policies and enacting laws geared towards national development yet in alignment with international minimum standards. For example, the preservation of Africa's vast and diverse cultural traditions is vital to its legal reforms. Protecting geographical indications and cultural expressions through IP mechanisms is not merely a legal or economic necessity but a crucial act of cultural preservation and empowerment. In this context, IP law becomes a powerful tool for safeguarding African identity, promoting local economic development, and resisting the homogenising forces of globalisation.

Recent developments in protecting traditional knowledge exemplify the evolving nature of IP law in Africa. The Treaty on Intellectual Property, Genetic Resources, and Associated Traditional Knowledge marks a significant step forward in recognising and protecting the rights of indigenous peoples and local communities. This Treaty mandates the disclosure of the origin of genetic resources in patent applications, ensuring that the contributions of indigenous knowledge systems are both acknowledged and respected. It is crucial to acknowledge and appreciate these knowledge systems as they are invaluable to our understanding of the world. The Treaty's provisions, which intersect IP law with broader access and benefit-sharing issues, represent a critical shift towards a more equitable international IP regime. The recognition of traditional knowledge associated with genetic resources as a valuable asset in scientific research and innovation further illustrates this evolution. The consensus approval of the treaty in Geneva, following negotiations that began in 2001, highlights the growing international recognition of the need to protect these knowledge systems from exploitation and ensure their fair integration into global innovation ecosystems.

Regional organisations such as the African Regional Intellectual Property Organization (ARIPO) and the Organisation Africaine de la Propriété Intellectuelle (OAPI) play a pivotal role in harmonising IP laws across the continent. Although these frameworks contain significant differences, they have continued to explore bilateral cooperation in their responses. Their efforts in standardising and coordinating IP regulations are crucial for fostering an environment conducive to innovation, attracting foreign investment, and facilitating cross-border cooperation.

Intellectual property rights (IPRs) are fundamental to innovation, providing creators and inventors with the legal protections necessary to commercialise their ideas. A robust IP regime incentivises innovation across various sectors, contributes to economic growth, and enhances competitiveness. For Africa, establishing a supportive IP environment is essential for fostering innovation and positioning the continent as a key player in the global economy. The significance of IPR extends beyond economic considerations, playing a vital role in the social and cultural domains. The African Union's initiatives, such as the Continental Strategy on Geographical Indications (2017) and the African Model Legislation for the Protection of the Rights of Local Communities and Breeders (2000), reflect a growing awareness of the need to protect Africa's biological and cultural diversity. These instruments aim to regulate access to genetic resources, ensure fair benefit-sharing, and protect the rights of local communities, thereby supporting sustainable development and food security.

Africa is at a critical juncture in its legal development concerning IP and technology. There is an urgent need to protect indigenous knowledge, cultural expressions, and biodiversity through context-specific IP laws while also addressing the demands of the digital economy through comprehensive technology regulations. This dual challenge requires

African nations to adopt a nuanced and multifaceted approach to legal reform, considering the unique contexts and challenges faced by different countries across the continent. The continent's technological and economic transformation, which has accelerated in recent years, both drives and is driven by increased IP creation. Although African countries vary widely in political, historical, and systemic contexts, the overarching trend points to a rise in innovation. This trend underscores the importance of both African and international stakeholders in considering the implications of these advancements for IP creation, exploitation, and protection.

In the realm of technology law, Africa faces both opportunities and challenges as it navigates rapid advancements in digital technologies. Historically, the continent's approach to technology regulation has been reactive, often lagging behind technological change. Outside of Asia, Africa's young population is the dominant force on the internet. Beyond its growing spending power, Africa has become a hub for innovation and experimentation. However, the experience of the COVID-19 pandemic revealed that the apparent progress in mobile internet penetration might have been misleading. Access to technology remains uneven, with both intra- and inter-digital divides persisting across African countries. This realisation has highlighted the need for proactive and forward-looking regulatory frameworks that can support the digital economy's development while safeguarding citizens' rights and interests.

Regarding the adoption and utilisation of technology, there are concerted efforts from African leadership to ensure that the continent maximises the benefits of the fourth industrial revolution. The production of the Digital Transformation Strategy for Africa by the African Union Commission in conjunction with the UN Economic Commission for Africa, Smart Africa, AUDANEPAD, Regional Economic Communities, African Development Bank, Africa Telecommunications Union, Africa Capacity Building Foundation, International Telecommunication Union, and the World Bank is geared towards a common and coordinated approach. The Digital Transformation Strategy aims to harness digital technologies and innovation to transform African societies and economies to promote Africa's integration, break the digital divide, and ensure Africa's ownership of modern tools of digital management. Even with this, it took almost a decade for the African Union Convention on Cyber Security and Personal Data Protection to enter into force since 2014 it was adopted. Nonetheless, African countries are increasingly addressing critical issues such as data protection, cybersecurity, and digital governance. While leading nations like Kenya, Nigeria, and South Africa have made significant strides in establishing comprehensive legal frameworks, a substantial gap remains between the most and least developed countries regarding legislative progress and enforcement capabilities. Bridging this gap is essential to ensure that all African nations can fully participate in the digital economy and benefit from technological advancements. The potential of IP and technology law to drive development in Africa is immense. By leveraging IPR protections, African businesses can create, commercialise, and secure revenue from innovative products and services. Patents, trademarks, and copyrights provide avenues for African companies to gain competitive advantages in both domestic and international markets, attracting investment and fostering economic growth. The success of companies like Nigeria's SecureID and Kenya's BRCK demonstrates how innovative African firms can leverage IP to build sustainable businesses and secure global partnerships.

As African businesses continue to make their mark on the global stage, it is imperative that they manage and protect their IP effectively. This will enable them to expand into new markets, create employment opportunities, enhance competitiveness, and engage in strategic partnerships. Furthermore, the role of IP in addressing critical issues such as poverty, food security, and water management cannot be overstated. Innovations in these areas, protected by robust IP regimes, can potentially transform lives across the continent.

Several key factors will shape the future of IP and technology law in Africa. The African Continental Free Trade Area (AfCFTA) can significantly influence IP law, particularly in cross-border enforcement and the protection of regional products. Additionally, the ongoing digital transformation, accelerated by the COVID-19 pandemic, will continue to drive the need for adaptable and robust technology laws. For IP and technology law to effectively support sustainable development in Africa, future reforms must be inclusive, considering the diverse needs of all stakeholders, including small and medium enterprises, indigenous communities, and the informal sector. Furthermore, strengthening the capacity of legal institutions and enforcement agencies will be crucial for effectively implementing and enforcing these laws.

A nuanced and strategic approach is required to fully realise the potential of IP and technology in supporting Africa's sustainable development. This includes developing IP policies aligned with national development goals, investing in IP education and awareness, promoting public-private partnerships, and ensuring equitable access to patented technologies. By doing so, Africa can harness the power of innovation to drive economic growth, social development, and cultural preservation, shaping a future that reflects the continent's rich heritage and dynamic potential.

This edited collection begins with Afolashade Adewunmi's exploration of how intangible cultural heritage can be protected amidst rapid technological advancement. Adewunmi critically examines the adequacy of existing IP frameworks, such as copyright, in safeguarding intangible cultural heritage, highlighting the risks posed by globalisation and technological change. The chapter underscores the importance of protecting traditional cultural expressions (TCEs) from misappropriation, particularly in the digital age, where technology has exacerbated such misappropriation, often without any benefits accruing to the original communities.

Following this, Ibijoke Byron addresses preserving traditional knowledge under a sui generis regime in Nigeria. Byron's chapter critically analyses the protection of traditional knowledge within the framework of customary and international law, focusing on the challenges posed by the depletion of biological resources and the consequent loss of indigenous livelihoods. The chapter advocates for the urgent enactment of sui generis legislation in Nigeria to ensure the effective protection of traditional knowledge and the rights of indigenous communities.

Nikolai Milogolov and Azamat Berberov's chapter on digital tax reform for Africa discusses the complexities of formulating international tax policies suitable for the continent's unique circumstances. They critically assess the evolving nature of digitalisation in African economies and argue for a tailored approach to tax reform that considers the diverse economic and digital capacities of African states. Their analysis suggests policy proposals that balance the need for global cooperation with the protection of Africa's economic and fiscal interests.

Helen Chuma-Okoro and Ifeoma Oluwasemilore then introduce the theme of COVID-19 into the IP-technology dialogue, examining the intersection of IPRs, agricultural biotechnology, and food security in Nigeria. Their chapter critically evaluates the role of IP in enhancing food self-sufficiency, particularly in the context of the pandemic, and offers recommendations for strengthening Nigeria's IP framework to support sustainable agricultural development.

Finally, Bukola Faturoti examines the state of internet access and online learning during the COVID-19 pandemic, focusing on the implications for education in Africa. Faturoti's chapter critically assesses the strategies employed by African governments to sustain access to education during the pandemic, highlighting the challenges of unequal access to technology and the internet. The chapter concludes with recommendations for future policy strategies to bridge the digital divide and ensure that more Africans can benefit from online education.

Africa stands at a pivotal juncture, poised for a transformation that could redefine its role on the global stage. The intersection of IP and technology law presents an unparalleled opportunity to address the continent's historical challenges and shape a future of innovation, equity, and cultural resurgence. The difficulties rooted in colonial legacies and global inequalities are undeniable but not insurmountable. The current momentum of legal reform and technological advancement offers a unique chance to transcend these barriers and chart a course toward a prosperous and just future.

This collection of essays is more than an academic exploration; it is a powerful call to action. The insights and strategies articulated within these pages are essential frameworks for designing policies that will propel Africa into a new era of growth and leadership. These discussions are not merely retrospective analyses; they are forward-looking visions that challenge us to reimagine Africa's future—a future where the continent not only overcomes the vestiges of its past but also leads the world in innovation and resilience. The urgency of this moment cannot be overstated. The decisions we make today will determine whether Africa can fully harness the opportunities of the digital age, leverage its vast cultural and intellectual resources, and achieve sustainable and inclusive development. This is not just a moment of reflection but a moment of action, demanding bold thinking, visionary leadership, and an unwavering commitment to progress.

As you explore the literature presented in this volume, consider it not merely as a collection of scholarly works but as a blueprint for the future. These discussions are intended to inspire and equip you with the knowledge and strategies necessary to contribute actively to Africa's advancement. The potential for progress is immense, and the stakes are profound, but with the right approach and a collective will, Africa can move beyond reflection on its past to actively shape its future. This challenge demands an optimistic and determined outlook coupled with a forward-thinking vision. The future of Africa is not merely a possibility—it is a shared responsibility. By engaging with the ideas and strategies discussed in this book, we can collectively work towards a future where Africa thrives and sets a compelling example for the rest of the world.

Protecting intangible cultural heritage in the era of rapid technological advancement

Afolasade A. Adewumi

ABSTRACT

Globalisation and social transformation have impinged upon Intangible Cultural Heritage (ICH) which is the foundation on which a nation's identity and knowledge is built. Safeguarding and protecting it, therefore, is beneficial to understanding the present and charting the way forward for the future identities and development. Traditional Cultural Expressions (TCE) have over time suffered from misappropriation by the actions of people outside a traditional community. The development of technology has greatly enhanced this misappropriation on a world-wide scale with no benefits accruing to the traditional communities that originally own the expressions. With COVID 19 lockdown and social distancing, several sectors of the society have moved on to the use of technology to ensure that they remain relevant as technological advancement through scientific progress is a way of expressing the right to cultural life. This article appraised ICH, the problems of protection and focussed on Nigeria using traditional craftmanship as a case study. The article proffered modalities for safeguarding, most especially in this era of technological advancement amidst COVID-19 pandemic.

1. Introduction

The existence of human beings over time has found expression in oral tradition such as songs, poetry, tales, stories, indigenous knowledge with language serving as the vehicle of transmission from generation to generation (Cornu 2020). Every culture symbolises an unequalled body of values that cannot be substituted because of their uniqueness (Adewumi 2013). In pre-colonial Africa, this creativity was respected and regarded as part of human civilisation (Arowolo 2019). Communal rights were recognised and protected alongside individual ownership rights (Elias 1956).

With technological development paving way for globalisation (Sengupta 2001), many people in developing countries like Nigeria, have abandoned their culture and language in a bid to embrace the foreign culture of the colonial masters. This led to the abandonment of customary laws protecting communal rights over indigenous knowledge among others. The Cultural Policy for Nigeria[1] states that *Culture is not merely a return to the customs of the past. It embodies the attitude of a people to the future of their traditional values faced with the demands of modern technology which is an essential factor of development and progress.*' This provision depicts that the past way of doing things is not to be jettisoned in a bid to embrace modernity.

The Intangible Cultural Heritage (ICH) Convention is the result of the international community reflecting on the cultural consequences of pursuing modernity. Oral tradition should not be allowed to become extinct so that generations yet unborn will not be disadvantaged in respect of their cultural inheritance (Blake 2015).[2] All over the world, traditions and customary practices have been disappearing at an alarming rate with the use of western standards as the yardstick for regulating non-western cultures. The initiative brought about by the Intangible Heritage Convention is aimed at ensuring that traditional cultures that do not flout human rights principles but have been neglected, ignored, or rejected by the modern-day governments are preserved from extinction by the modern governments (Blake 2009).

Heritage refers to assets that have been passed down from one generation to another or items of cultural significance either tangible or intangible.[3] Heritage is as old as humanity (Lowenthal 1997). Cultural heritage is a symbol of the cultural identity of a self-identified group, be it a nation or a people, and an essential element in the construction of that group's identity (Blake 2000). WIPO puts it 'as the forms in which traditional culture is expressed'.[4]

ICH has been defined by the Convention on the Safeguarding of the ICH to cover cultural practices, representations, expressions, knowledge, skills- as well as the instruments, objects, artefacts, and cultural spaces used for the performance of cultural activities (Adewumi 2018). Communities' regenerate intangible heritage in response to their relationship with their environment culminating in an identity different from that of another community. This cultural diverseness and ingeniousness need to be respected and promoted in as much as they are not contrary to existing international human rights instruments and enjoy cooperating admiration among the different communities, groups, and individuals. The intangible heritage must also be such that enjoys authenticity.[5]

In its definition, the Convention classifies intangible heritage into five domains namely: oral traditions and expressions including language as a vehicle of the ICH; performing arts; social practices, rituals and festive events; knowledge and practices concerning nature and the universe; traditional craftsmanship.[6] Each country is left with the duty of determining what qualifies and needs protection within its territory as the Convention on the Safeguarding of the ICH 2003, did not spell out the identification and context of the ICH. The duty of safeguarding the heritage lies with the communities. Blake has referred to safeguarding as 'fostering the conditions within which it [the ICH] can continue to be created, maintained and transmitted' (Blake 2009).

Intangible heritage helps to enrich cultural diversity and human creativity. The expressions of intangible heritage give an insight into the worldviews of a community (Okumu 2016). This makes heritage very germane to achieving sustainable development in any society. Development cannot be separated from man's culture. Life revolves around culture and religion. Culture makes a man and man cannot be developed in vacuum (Owete and Oviomaigho 2016). Osagie has defined development to encompass '... the qualitative and quantitative positive transformation of the lives of a people that does not only enhance their material well-being but also ensure their social well-being, including the restoration of human dignity' (Osagie 1985).

Heritage is preserved for reasons chiefly of which are cultural memory, distance facilities, environmental diversity, and economic benefits (Prompayuk and Chairattananon 2016). Over time, researchers have expressed concerns about some aspects of intangible heritage becoming extinct if not safeguarded. It has been extrapolated that the last elderly person with the full command of a native language dies fortnightly. This culminates in inferring that by the year 2100, about 2500 out of the 6000 languages in the world would have been lost (Okumu 2016).

The new normal all over the world caused by the COVID-19 pandemic has prevented people from physically relating with each other in large groups as obtained during cultural and social events. Moreover, it has been established that the death rate because of the virus is high among the elderly because many of them have existing underlying medical conditions. The elderly in this case happens to be custodian of intangible heritage. There is therefore the need to ensure cultural life does not become a thing of the past as life adjusts to the new normal of social distancing and reliance on technological advancement for survival.

This article is divided into seven parts, the first being this introduction. The second part discusses globalisation and its impact on intangible heritage. The third part appraises the attempt to protect intangible heritage with existing laws. The fourth part discusses the Convention on the safeguarding of the ICH 2003 while the fifth part considers how far Nigeria has fared in protecting Intangible heritage through the 2003 convention using traditional craftsmanship as a case study. The sixth part is the conclusion.

2. Westernisation, globalisation, and its impact on intangible heritage

African development before colonialism was hinged on the heritage of brotherhood and communal living, work ethics and sound morality. Communal rights/group rights existing over customary practices were patterned along social groups or kinship associated with the practices, with contravention of norms attracting strict sanctions ranging from fines to sacrifices imposed either by the king, chief, head of family, group, or clan (Morris 1966; Kludze 1973; Driberg 1970).

Rights over literary, artistic and musical works were socially acknowledged and financially rewarded while charlatans were not spared but dealt with accordingly (Arowolo 2019). Claims over rights between communities were settled through fighting or by negotiations. Spiritual ownership over tangible and intangible property was believed to reside in the ancestors and gods/deities (Arowolo 2019).[7] Taboos were the means of protecting traditional intellectual property, as it translates to the wrath of God being visited on whoever commits a breach of a norm culminating in the death penalty (Farran 2014). The fear of attracting the wrath of the gods prevented a breach of the taboo. The value of taboos as a source of an ethical control and societal regulation is strengthened because, with its use, justice is perceived to be quicker (Osei 2006).

During the colonial era, the British colonial masters did not pay attention to the rich Nigerian culture and heritage. The traditions, language, norms, and values were made to appear inferior to western education and culture (Adewumi and Olatunbosun 2015). The tangible aspects of heritage were carted away as curios to museums abroad which led to the abandonment of some of the practices and representations that give meaning to those objects (Adewumi 2015; 2019). Customary practices and laws were subjected to the validity tests based on western standards and many of them were adjudged to be repugnant and jettisoned (Arowolo 2019). As Gbolokom succinctly puts it '... colonialists categorically denied the existence of African cultural values and worse still, taught the Africans to despise them' (Mbakogu 2004).

Westernisation came with a change in the lifestyle, political and cultural ideology of societies leading to the altering of the lived experiences of the colonised territories. The villages were emptied as people left to seek better lives elsewhere. Many had to reject the traditional or old which was regarded as being backward or crude in favour of the modern or the western way of life (Gao, Zhang, and Long 2017). Disappointedly, the traditional culture was regarded as subservient and inferior where any part of them were retained. Cultural differences thus became a tool for creating boundaries, exclusions, and conflicts in the society.[8] However, there is a move towards reconsidering some of the traditional ways of doing things especially in areas where the western way has not been able to yield the results desired (Ekhator 2019; Adewumi and Ojuade 2019).

Globalisation, otherwise viewed as an outcome of advanced modernisation, modern capitalism, or imperialism (Sengupta 2001), has been embraced as the best way in achieving development. This can be attributed to the fact that most countries are led by the elites and technocrats who are not interested in considering alternatives (Guttal 2007). Sengupta[9] views globalisation as 'the fast-changing world events in the last one and half decades pointing towards the globe as an inclusive single place.' In other words, globalisation depicts the interconnectedness of the world.

Rather than being inclusive, globalisation created a kind of hegemony where social, cultural, ideological or economic influence is exerted on the developing countries by the developed countries bringing about imbalances between the rich and the poor.[10] Trade and financial liberalisation and privatisation have devastated the livelihoods of craftsmen, artisans, farmers, fishers, workers, and indigenous peoples the world over.[11] Artisans, craftsmen, workers, and indigenous communities have faced deep and shattering livelihood crises because of free trade and investment brought about by globalisation.[12] Globalisation has made even the younger generation not to be interested in learning about their cultural heritage and the knowledge it offers (Isa et al. 2018). They rather want to flow with the urban culture and technological advancement.

Rene Maheu's[13] statement in 1970 which goes thus is very apt:

> Man is the means and the end of development; he is not the one-dimensional abstraction of homo economics, but a living reality, a human person, in the infinite variety of his needs, his potentials and his aspirations ... in the concept of development the centre of gravity has thus shifted from the economic to the social, and we have reached a point where this shift begins to approach the cultural.

His statement has set the pace for where things stand today because it kickstarted the idea of culture taking a pride of place in policy making agenda (Owete and Oviomaigho).[14] For sustainable development to take place, the languages, marital practices, architecture, religion, music, dance, mutual social responsibility, communal living, traditional knowledge, structure and authority which form the cultural heritage of a people have to be revamped and inculcated into science and technology.

3. Attempts to protect intangible heritage through copyright law

Enjoying copyright protection is based on fulfilling certain requirements one of which is individual authorship that is alien to ICH (Antons 2013). The attempt at protecting heritage through copyright is an offshoot of the lack of international awareness on the need to protect and the lack of instruments protecting intangible heritage before the 1960s.[15] Intellectual Property and Human Rights have copiously discussed the nexus between indigenous knowledge and culture and copyright (Bowrey 2011). The fundamental difference between them is anchored on the divergence of values which intellectual property system tends to protect and the cardinal virtue of indigenous knowledge (Antons, Blakeney, and Heath 2004).[16]

Attempts at protecting folklore with copyright laws have been showcased in some international instruments. The Berne Convention empowers member states to protect unpublished works of unknown authors believed to originate from their territory.[17] The WIPO Tunis Model Law on Copyright for Developing Countries was the product of a collaboration between United Nations Educational, Scientific and Cultural Organization (UNESCO) and World Intellectual Property Organization (WIPO) in 1976. In 1985, UNESCO/WIPO Model Provisions for National Laws on the Protection of Expressions of Folklore Against Illicit Exploitation and other Forms of Prejudicial Actions came up. The Agreement on Trade-Related Aspects of Intellectual Property Rights [TRIPS][18] and the WIPO Copyright Treaty 1996 (WCT)[19] have incorporated Articles 1–21 of the Berne Convention. WIPO Performances and Phonograms Treaty 1996 (WPPT)[20] and regional instruments also provide protection for expressions of folklore (Ayoubi 2018) which like other instruments before it have not been adequate.

The framework of copyright protection has developed from a private law point of view which seeks to incentivise creativity. The cardinal requirements for copyright protection are framed from this standpoint, which then causes frictions if applied to ICH. Monetary incentives and individual intents and rights which underlie most copyright protection mechanisms are alien to the 'owners' of ICH. For context, an analysis of the key elements of copyright vis-à-vis ICH is carried out below (Kuruk 1999):

(1) Authorship: Identifying the specific source of ICH is often difficult, if not impossible. While it may be possible to trace authorship through oral history, findings from such may not be totally definitive. The concept of ICH is also linked to knowledge as 'heritage' as opposed to knowledge as 'property', thereby reflecting its custodianship and inter-generational character (Roy 2008; Nwabueze 2013).
(2) Originality: To afford protection to a 'work', copyright law requires that such work be original. Works that are not original are regarded as being in the public domain, and not eligible for protection. ICH has often developed over time.
(3) Fixation: Copyright often applies only fixed tangible medium of expression, while ICH is often not fixed.
(4) Duration: Copyright does not vest in an entity in perpetuity. Both local and international copyright laws put a limit on the number of years after the 'death' of an author or date of publication when the copyright will expire. This expiration element cannot work for the protection of ICH due to its inter-generational nature.

No date of publication can be easily identified and allowing for an expiration point will deprive future generations of the benefit of their heritage.

In Nigeria, the Copyright Act[21] is fashioned after the 1956 Copyright Act of Britain which has since been replaced by the Copyrights, Designs, and Patents Act, 1988. The Act is designed after the WIPO Tunis Model. Part II of the Act protects neighbouring rights, which are not copyright (Cornish and Llewelyn 2007) but are the work of performers and folklore as is obtainable under international best practice.[22] The Act[23] defines folklore to encompass the creation of a group which is tradition based, reflecting their identity and values and passed on orally or by imitation. It includes folklore, folk poetry, folk riddles, folk songs and instrumental music, folk dances and folk plays, etc. (Oriakhogba and Fenemigho 2014). The expressions mentioned in the Act do not include all aspects of intangible heritage. Scholars have also repeatedly mentioned the difficulty in enforcing the protection available to folklore under the Act (Adewopo 2006).

There is therefore no gainsaying that intellectual property laws are inadequate to protect ICH.

4. The Convention on the safeguarding of the ICH 2003

While opening the definition and meanings ascribed to the word 'heritage' (Duvelle 2014), the Convention seeks to protect heritage that has 'universal value.' One cannot but opine that universal value in this regard is based on a set of euro-centred values which is of western origin.

However, the hallmark of this convention is the fact that it has created a kind of self-awareness and self confidence in heritage practitioners all over the world and especially in developing countries to showcase and claim their cultures with pride while the different cultures become recognised, accepted and protected in the world context (Zhang 2017).

The idea of representativeness found in the Convention depicts that it is the community or its chosen organisation that must do the speaking and not someone else doing the speaking on their behalf. The speaker, hence, determines the culture that is representative of a community. Each community driving its own culture and propagating the goals to pursue and the values to protect.[24] However, community participation which is central to the 2003 Convention constitutes a major downside to its proper implementation.[25]

Article 11 of the Convention encapsulates that safeguarding ICH lies with the community who are to practise and transmit intangible heritage bearing in mind the human, social and cultural contexts in which the enactment of ICH occurs.[26] Blake has noted that the legal framework of most countries does not place emphasis on communal rights but on individual rights. International legal discussions however tend to agree that protecting individual rights ultimately guarantees group rights because individuals exist as members of certain groups which may be cultural, ethnic, or linguistic in nature.[27]

The 2003 Convention can be said to have provided the leeway for intangible heritage to be protected with the use of technological means. China in 2004 signed the Convention, passed the Intangible Heritage Law in 2011 and has 38 items listed in the world level in 2015. Safeguarding intangible heritage has moved from being a national issue to a social movement.[28] Many practices erstwhile considered a threat and potential danger for the practitioners now bring them honour, benefit and wealth.[29] China has been able to conquer cultural revolution. Officially recognising and protecting traditional cultures alongside modern cultures has created cultural cohesion among communities.[30]

Also, Kenya, a state party, has taken significant steps in protecting and safeguarding her intangible heritage. The government has put in place laws, policies, and other safeguarding measures including digitisation into use though not without encountering some challenges which do not however look insurmountable.[31]

5. Protection of intangible heritage at the national level

5.1 Case studies

The community educates the individual about the societal and cultural values which varies from one community to another. Sustainable development can therefore be said to be hinged on rural development with orientation starting and taking the form of community development. Poorna et al., while reiterating this point referred to case studies around the globe specifically from Venezuela, South Africa and the desert region of Western and Central Australia (Poorna, Mymoon, and Hariharan 2014).

In Venezuela, oral traditional knowledge in the Amazonian jungle has been documented through the BioZulua project. This project has documented the traditional agricultural technologies of the food crops and medicinal plants of the 24 ethnic groups found in the area with detailed information about their geographical locations and digital images. This database is however not available for public access but has been documented in readiness for future legal protection through a *sui generis* approach because it is seen as the intellectual property of the indigenous groups which copyright law cannot adequately protect (Muller 2004; Johnson 2002).[32]

In South Africa, there is an online indigenous knowledge database called the Ulwazi programme. Indigenous knowledge of the Durban area relating to traditional celebrations, clothing, Zulu proverbs, traditional agricultural methods, folk tales and spiritual herbs are collected in English and the Zulu languages by fieldworkers engaged to work closely with the community leaders and shared on the website in such a way that the information posted can be edited and improved upon by other users in an interactive manner. The Digital library of traditional knowledge forms a part of the local public library network and is owned by the communities while the library functions as the custodian of the knowledge (McNulty 2012).

Social cohesion is promoted by the knowledge sharing among the communities. The fieldworkers who are youths benefit from the computer skills they are trained in for recording audio and visual materials and uploading them unto the website. These computer skills help in their future employability. The availability of their heritage online has also attracted tourists to the Durban area. This method represents a framework where the community and the government work together in a well-organised manner to gather information on traditional knowledge though not in a manner that can be said to protect the knowledge because the knowledge is placed in open access that can be manipulated by anyone without validation.

In Anangu, an indigenous community in the desert region of Western and Central Australia there is the Ara Irititja project which is community owned and controlled and focuses on restoring cultural resources of different media including photographs, documents, films, videos, sound recordings, etc., held by public and private persons and bodies to the community. The prominent objective of the project is to store these resources basically originating from oral traditional knowledge in electronic format for posterity needs and long-term reference. The project however ensures proper archival and maintenance of the original resources from which the electronic database is created for reference purposes. The Ara Irititja creates an elaborate network outsourcing information about cultural resources and materials like names, stories and dates, from members of the community (Lowish 2008).[33] With the heritage information categorised into compartments, it forms a living archive constituting a response to the present needs of the community geared towards its development. This archive is protected by the Australian Copyright Law and the moral and intellectual rights are retained in the community depicting a *sui generis* approach.

Nigeria is a country where the cultural identity of an individual is rooted in the community he emanates from Oriakhogba and Fenemigho (2019) have noted in respect to Benin Bronze casting, that protecting it under copyright law will prevent the community from enjoying the economic benefit of the art as a group and advocated for an Intellectual property and Traditional Cultural Expression (TCE) framework that would make possible the enjoyment by the community of all benefits ascribable to trading in the art.

It is hereby submitted that the answer to this problem is in the implementation of the 2003 UNESCO Intangible Heritage Convention discussed in the preceding section.

5.2 Traditional craftsmanship as a case study

The COVID-19 lockdown greatly hampered social gathering and activities in every community. The media is replete with information that the older generation are most susceptible to COVID-19 deaths (Irfan and Belluz 2020). How will intangible heritage be safeguarded in these times knowing fully well that this heritage resides mainly in the elderly? Armed with this thought, the Heritage Protection Initiative, in the wake of the COVID-19 pandemic carried out a survey on the level of protection enjoyed by the intangible heritage domain of traditional craftmanship within Ibadan metropolis, located in Southwest Nigeria.

In respect of traditional craftsmanship in Ibadan, the largest city in West Africa, a visit was paid to the *'Agbede Adodo'* blacksmith compound in the ancient part of the Ibadan city at *Bere*. The blacksmiths in that compound are the descendants of the makers of the ammunition used for wars by the warriors of Ibadan. Ibadan's pre-colonial history is centred on militarism, imperialism, and violence.[34] In pre-colonial times, the men were recruited to fabricate weapons of war for the Ibadan warlords dating back to the days of the first *Aare Latoosa*. The blacksmiths were forbidden to be farmers therefore they are the only ones who do not lay claim to having an expanse of villages in what is known as Ibadan Less City area. They were mainly urbanised. Legend also has it that for them to be committed to the work of producing implements of war, most of them were eunuchs, forbidden to socialise with women.[35] History has it that was extraordinarily strong because the trade demands a lot of strength. Children born of women outside the compound were brought into the compound to learn the blacksmith trade.

With the aid of unstructured interviews conducted on the family members in the blacksmith compound, information was garnered to the effect that their trade is only for men that are extraordinarily strong. Many of the family members that are not strong enough to withstand the strenuous nature of the job end up learning other trades or taking up white-collar jobs but that is not to be interpreted to mean that they do not have an idea of how the process is carried out. The influx of commercially produced farm implements from overseas had a major negative impact on their trade as students preferred the fashionable cutlasses and hoes which were cheaper and not as heavy as the locally made ones. This made them reduce the quality and price of their products to attract sales. Westernisation and globalisation affected their trade as some implements, they manufacture are no longer needed due to technological advancement. With the Covid-19 lock down, many of them who do not have the strength to carry on with the blacksmith trade have had to return home to the family compound because their other trades and vocations were not enjoying patronage.

In ensuring that their family trade does not become extinct, they are of the opinion that the government should come to their aid and showcase traditional craftsmanship in a sustainable manner. Teaching of traditional crafts can be incorporated into the primary and secondary schools' curriculum and members of the families practising these trades can be called upon from time to time to introduce the trade to the youths. This stance reiterates the fact that the right to cultural life as provided for in section 15(1)(a) of the International Covenant on Economic, Social, and Cultural (ICESCR)[36] involves the right of access to one's culture, that is, the right to know one's own culture and that of others through education and information (Adewumi 2021). This right is one of the rights children are entitled to under the Child's Rights Act.[37] Adewumi and Olatunbosun (2015) have canvassed that Child's Rights have no meaning in the absence of a cultural identity.

Furthermore, the processes and knowledge of their trade are not documented in any form but learnt through observation and experience. When asked if they are willing to document their processes and even digitise them, they were elated but expressed their lack of funds and technical know-how to ensure the proper preservation of their indigenous knowledge is achieved. Their response, though an intelligent one to overcome their present challenge is fraught with its own challenges. Biyela, Oyelude, and Haumba (2016) have found that digitisation of indigenous knowledge by heritage institutions is almost non-existent in Nigeria. As noted by Sithole (2007); Akinwale (2012) and Dewah and Feni-Fete (2014), heritage institutions, in a bid to digitise traditional knowledge have been frustrated by lack of or insufficient funding; digital rights management; the complexity of ownership protocols; loss or misappropriation of digitised Indigenous Knowledge; lack or limited skills; inadequate infrastructure; lack of resources and unreliability of the preservation media. These challenges, it is believed, can be surmounted with adequate planning/coordination and funding.

The positive responses obtained from the family members interacted with maybe because they are exposed to western education and are able to appreciate the need to preserve heritage in a manner that will be sustainable and acceptable to the future generation. Their responses also buttress the fact that intangible heritage aids development as portrayed in the case studies discussed above. Hence the need to document them for posterity.

6. Way forward

The African Charter on Human and Peoples Rights[38] places the duty of protecting traditional values of the community on the African state and places on the individual, a concomitant duty of strengthening positive African cultural values in his relationship with other members of the society.[39] Nigerian heritage practitioners, therefore, need to be aware through sensitisation campaigns, especially at the community level, that the knowledge and skills kept in their memory should be digitised to prevent extinction. Digitisation[40] being a popular modern process of codification of information or knowledge to ensure accessibility globally and over a long period of time. Though projects for digitisation are limited in Africa, that is not enough excuse to leave things the way they are.

Intangible heritage can be collected in manuscript notebooks, questionnaire responses, photographs, oral recording, and digitisation to prevent extinction just as was carried out in the Ara Ititja project. The heritage collected in a tangible form can be protected as a material culture for future generations. Language being the tool of communication, Nigerian languages need to be developed consciously so they can have a pride of place in the global revolution, hastened by the prevailing COVID-19 pandemic, or become obsolete. The government can start by making the dominant languages in each state the official language of communication in the states.

To avoid misappropriation of intangible heritage, Nigeria must focus on inventorying and documenting as the first step towards digitisation of the records. If this is done, issues of origin of the material in cases of application for patent, prior informed consent of the owners and other issues of misappropriation will be checkmated. The procedure adopted in the case study utilised by the Anangu community is prescribed as a starting point in documenting Nigeria's traditional knowledge.

At this juncture, it cannot be overemphasised that Nigeria must stop blaming the present situation of lack of adequate protection for heritage on the past injustice and take steps towards contributing her quota of showcasing cultural diversity to the global community's creativity through safeguarding her intangible heritage and ensuring adequate representation of them through the 2003 Convention platform.

The wheel of digitising information on ICH can however be clogged by low community participation in the digitisation process; low technical know-how about how best to carry out the process; inadequate policy about intellectual property rights relating to traditional knowledge and insufficient commitment from stakeholders, among others. The government, therefore, needs to put mechanisms in place to address these issues through manpower training and community enlightenment.

7. Conclusion

It is noteworthy that the government of Nigeria has not been seen to take heritage issues with the seriousness it deserves. There is no national legislation on protecting intangible heritage though the country is a signatory to the 2003 UNESCO Convention neither can it be said that adequate structures exist for safeguarding intangible heritage at the community level. Nigeria has no indigenous language elevated to the level of a national language.

Since each culture has a dignity and value which must be respected and preserved' and 'every people have the right and the duty to develop its culture',[41] the Nigerian government needs to take safeguarding cultural heritage as a priority issue that should become not just a national project but a social movement involving everyone. Legitimate status should be given to otherwise suppressed cultures by enacting the Intangible Heritage Law.

Notes

1. Cultural Policy for Nigeria 1988. Part 1, Preamble 1.3
2. Statement by Kochoiro Matsuura in 2008 when he was the Director General of UNESCO.
3. Heritage and Cultural Property Crime National Policing Strategic Assessment 2013. United Kingdom. Retrieved 19 July 2020 from http://www.museumsassociation.org/download?id=1038797
4. WIPO. 'Traditional cultural expressions'. Available: http://www.wipo.int/tk/en/folklore/.
5. Convention on the safeguarding of the Intangible Cultural Heritage 2003, Article 1
6. *Ibid.* Article 2
7. *citing* S. Kasere, 'Campfire Zimbabwe's Tradition of Caring' 6(2) *Voice of Africa*. United Nations Non-Governmental Liaison Service.
8. *Ibid.* 178
9. Sengupta C, *op. cit.* at 3137
10. *ibid.* 528
11. *ibid.* 529
12. *ibid.*
13. Rene Maheu, then UNESCO Director-General's message to the world at The Intergovernmental Conference on the Administrative and Financial aspects of Cultural Policies held in Venice in 1970.
14. at 121
15. The Conventions and Instruments that relate to protecting intangible heritage came into force thus: Convention (No. 107) Concerning the Protection and Integration of Indigenous and other Tribal and Semi-Tribal Populations in Independent Countries 328 UNTS 247 (opened for signature 26 June 1957, entered into force 2 June 1959); Convention for the Safeguarding of the Intangible Cultural Heritage 2368 UNTS 3 (adopted on 17 October 2003, entered into force 20 April 2006); Convention on the Protection and Promotion of the Diversity of Cultural Expression 2440 UNTS 311 (adopted on 20 October 2005, entered into force 18 March 2007); United Nations Declaration on the Rights of Indigenous Peoples GA Res 61/295 A/Res/61/295 (2007) [UNDRIP].
16. See the book generally on intellectual property harmonisation in Asia Pacific.
17. Berne Convention for the Protection of Literary and Artistic Works 1161 UNTS 31 (opened for signature 9 September 1886, entered into force 5 December 1887), art 15(4) [Berne Convention].
18. The Agreement on Trade-Related Aspects of Intellectual Property Rights 1869 UNTS 299 (adopted 15 April 1994, entered into force 1 January 1995) [TRIPS]
19. WIPO Copyright Treaty 2186 UNTS 121 (opened for signature 20 December 1996, entered into force 6 March 2002), art 1(4) [WCT]; Berne Convention, above n 17, arts 1–21.
20. WIPO Performances and Phonograms Treaty 2186 UNTS 203 (adopted 20 December 1996, entered into force 20 May 2002) [WPPT]
21. Copyright Decree 47 of 1988 now Copyright Act 1988.
22. The Rome Convention for Protection of Performers, and Producers of Phonograms and Broadcasting Organisations and WIPO/UNESCO initiative on protection of folklore.
23. Copyright Act, s.31(5) (a-d)
24. Convention on the safeguarding of the Intangible Cultural Heritage 2003, Article 1(b)&(c)
25. Duvelle 2014, *op.cit.* at 33

26. Blake J. ' … The Implications of Community Involvement in 'Safeguarding' *op.cit.* 51
27. *ibid.* 53
28. Gao B, Zhang J and Long B. *op.cit.* at 168
29. *ibid.* at 169
30. *ibid* at 178
31. For a detailed account of steps taken by Kenya, see Okumu O. S. *op.cit.*
32. Rooting out Biopiracy, Down to Earth, 15 November 2002
33. Cited by Poorna, Mymoon, and Hariharan 2014 *op.cit*
34. Kriesi, History of Ibadan. Retrieved 19 July 2020 from https://ccii.ng/history-of-ibadan/
35. An account of the history of the *'Agbede Adodo'* compound was recounted by Prof. Remi Raji-Oyelade, one of the Mogaji's of Ibadan land representing the Adegboro compound during my interaction with him on the 19th day of July 2020, after the visit to the blacksmiths.
36. ICESCR, General Comment 21, para. 15 discusses the three components of this right, one of which is the right of access to one's culture.
37. Child Rights Act 2003, Cap. C50 Laws of the Federation of Nigeria 2004
38. The African Charter on Human and Peoples Rights, Article 17 para 3
39. *ibid* Article 29(7)
40. Biyela N, Oyelude A and Haumba E. *op. cit.*
41. UNESCO General Conference Declaration of 1966, Article 1

Disclosure statement

No potential conflict of interest was reported by the author(s).

ORCID

Afolasade A. Adewumi http://orcid.org/0000-0001-8503-7029

References

Adewopo, A. 2006. "Protection and Administration of Folklore in Nigeria." *Journal of Scottish Center for Research in Intellectual Property and Technologies* 3 (1): 1.

Adewumi, A. A. 2013. "Special Rights for the Development of Indigenous Peoples (IPs) in Africa: Any Need in a Democratic Society with Functional Human Rights Document?" *Nnamdi Azikiwe University Journal of International Law and Jurisprudence (NAUJILJ)* 4: 19–30.

Adewumi, A. A. 2021. "COVID-19 Pandemic and the Enjoyment of the Right to Cultural Life in Nigeria." *Art Antiquity and Law* XXVI (1): 73.

Adewumi, A. A. 2015. "Possessing Possession: Who Owns Benin Artefacts?" *Art, Antiquity and Law* XX (3): 229–242.

Adewumi, A. A. 2018. "Afrobeat Music as Cultural Heritage in Nigeria: Myth or Reality?" *Rivers' State University Journal of Public Law (R/S UJPL)* 5: 214–232.

Adewumi, A. A. 2019. "Benin Objects: Return of Stolen Objects or Restitution of Objects of Cultural Value?" *International Review of Law and Jurisprudence (IRLJ)* 1 (2): 177–182.

Adewumi, A. A., and S. U. Ojuade. 2019. "Customary Arbitration: An Effective way of Managing Child Maintenance Cases in law Clinics Unconnected with Courts." *UNIMAID Journal of Private and Property Law* 4 (1): 9–17.

Adewumi, A., and A. I. Olatunbosun. 2015. "Child's Rights Without Cultural Identity: A Mirage." *Justice Journal* 7: 116–137.

Akinwale, A. A. 2012. "Digitisation of Indigenous Knowledge for Natural Resources Management in Africa." Proceedings of the AERN Summit Paper Presented at the 20th Anniversary Summit of the African Educational Research Network at North Carolina State University, Raleigh, USA, 19 May, 1–18.

Antons, C. 2013. "At the Crossroads: The Relationship Between Heritage and Intellectual Property in Traditional Knowledge Protection in Southeast Asia." *Law in Context* 29 (1): 74–94.

Antons, C., M. Blakeney, and C. Heath. 2004. *Intellectual Property Harmonisation Within ASEAN and APEC*. The Hague: Kluwer Law International.

Arowolo, A. L. 2019. "African Traditional Intellectual Property Rights, Customary Law, and Legal Pluralism." *African Journal of Legal Studies* 11 (4): 299–318.

Ayoubi, L. 2018. "Copyright Harmonisation in the Asian Pacific Region: Weaving the Peoples Together?" In *Making Copyright Work for the Asian Pacific*, edited by S. Corbett, and J. C. Lai, 62, Australian National University Press.

Biyela, N., A. Oyelude, and E. Haumba. 2016. "Digital preservation of Indigenous Knowledge (IK) by Cultural Heritage Institutions: A comparative study of Nigeria, South Africa and Uganda". Accessed 29 June 2021. https://www.researchgate.net/publication/302430818_Digital_preservation_of_Indigenous_Knowledge_IK_by_Cultural_Heritage_Institutions_A_comparative_study_of_Nigeria_South_Africa_and_Uganda.

Blake, J. 2000. "On Defining the Cultural Heritage." *The International and Comparative Law Quarterly* 49 (1): 61–85.

Blake, J. 2015. *Cultural Heritage Intangible Aspects, in Blake J. International Cultural Heritage Law*, 150. New York: Oxford University Press.

Blake, J. 2009. "UNESCO's 2003 Convention on Intangible Cultural Heritage: The Implications of Community Involvement in 'Safeguarding'." In *Intangible Heritage*, edited by L. Smith, and N. Akagawa, 45–73. New York, NY: Routledge.

Bowrey, K. 2011. "Indigenous Culture, Knowledge and Intellectual Property: The Need for a New Category of Rights." In *Emerging Challenges in Intellectual Property*, edited by K. Bowrey, M. Handler, and D. Nicole, 46. Oxford: Oxford University Press.

Cornish, W., and D. Llewelyn. 2007. *Intellectual Property: Patents, Copyright, Trademarks and Allied Rights*, 375. London: Sweet and Maxwell.

Cornu, M. 2020. "Defining the Perimeter of the Intangible Cultural Heritage: Focus on Language." In *Intangible Cultural Heritage Under National Law and International Law Going Beyond the 2003 UNESCO Convention*, edited by M. Cornu, A. Vaivade, L. Martinet, and C. Hance, 54–67. Edward Edgar Publishing. Accessed 23 June 2021. https://www.elgaronline.com/view/edcoll/9781839100024/9781839100024.00012.xml.

Dewah, P., and V. Feni-Fete. 2014. "Issues and Prospects of Digitising Liberation Movements' Archives Held at the University of Fort Hare." *South Africa. Journal of the South African Society of Archivists* 47: 77–88.

Driberg, J. H. 1970. "The African Conception of Law." In *Readings in African Law*, edited by E. Cotran, and N. N. Rubin, 166. London: Frank Cass and Co.

Duvelle, C. 2014. "A Decade of Implementation of the Convention for the Safeguarding of the Intangible Cultural Heritage Challenges and Perspectives." *Ethnologies* 36 (1–2): 27–46. Retrieved 29 June 2021 from doi:10.7202/1037598ar.

Ekhator, E. 2019. "Traditional Oath-Taking as an Anti-Corruption Strategy in Nigeria." In *Combating the Challenges of Corruption in Nigeria: A Multidisciplinary Conversation*, edited by A. Agada, 323–324. Awka: Nigeria: Black Towers Publishers.

Elias, T. O. 1956. *The Nature of African Law*, 164. Manchester: Manchester University Press.

Farran, S. 2014. "Aid, Trade and Taboo: The Place of Indigenous Traditional Knowledge in Development Strategies: A Pacific Perspective." *Development Studies Research* 1 (1): 2.

Gao, B., J. Zhang, and B. Long. 2017. "The Social Movement of Safeguarding Intangible Cultural Heritage and the End of Cultural Revolutions in China." *Western Folklore* 76 (2): 167–180. Special Issue: Intangible Cultural Heritage in China (Spring 2017).

Guttal, S. 2007. "Globalisation." *Development in Practice* 17 (4–5): 523–553.

Irfan, U., and J. Belluz. 2020. "Why Covid-19 is so dangerous for older adults." Accessed 19 July 2020. https://www.vox.com/2020/3/12/21173783/coronavirus-death-age-covid-19-elderly-seniors.

Isa, W. M., N. A. Zin, F. Rosdi, and H. M. Sarim. 2018. "Digital Preservation of Intangible Cultural Heritage." *Indonesian Journal of Electrical Engineering and Computer Science* 12 (3): 1373–1379.

Johnson, O. 2002. "Venezuelan Project Establishes Indigenous Plant Database." *British Medical Journal* 325: 183.

Kludze, A. K. P. 1973. "Ghana – Ewe Law of Property." In *School of Oriental and African Studies Restatement of African Law*, edited by A. N. Allot. London: Sweet and Maxwell.

Kuruk, P. 1999. "Protecting Folklore Under Modern Intellectual Property Regimes: A Reappraisal of the Tensions Between Individual and Communal Rights in Africa and the United States." *American University Law Review* 48 (4): 776.

Lowenthal, D. 1997. *The Heritage Crusade and the Spoils of History*, 1. Harmondsworth, UK: Viking.

Lowish, S. 2008. "Ara Irititja: Adding More Value to Aboriginal art Through Education." *SangSaeng* 20: 8–11.

Mbakogu, I. A. 2004. "Is There Really a Relationship Between Culture and Development?." *Kamla-Ray Anthropologist* 6 (1): 27–43.

McNulty, N. 2012. "How to Build an Indigenous Digital Library Through Community Participation: the Case of the Ulwazi Programme." Proceedings of the standing Conference of eastern, Central and southern African library and information associations (SCECSAL), Nairobi, 400–411.

Morris, H. F. 1966. *The British Commonwealth: Uganda the Development of its Laws and Constitutions*, 237. London: Steven and sons.

Muller, M. R. 2004. "An analysis of the implications of intellectual property rights (IPR) on the Global Biodiversity Information Facility (GBIF)." 33, Accessed 29 June 2021. http://dlc.dlib.indiana.edu/dlc/handle/ 10535/3831.

Nwabueze, J. 2013. "The Role of Intellectual Property in Safeguarding Intangible Cultural Heritage in Museums." *International Journal of Intangible Heritage* 8: 181–190. Accessed 29 June 2021. https://www.ijih.org/volumes/article/436.

Okumu, O. S. 2016. "The Concept of Intangible Cultural Heritage in Kenya." In *Conservation of Natural and Cultural Heritage in Kenya* (vol. 50), edited by A. Deisser, and M. Njuguna, 45–58. London: UCL Press. Retrieved 23 June 2021 from http://www.jstor.com/stable/j.ctt1gxxpc6.10

Oriakhogba, D. O., A. I. Fenemigho, et al. 2019. "Exploring the Intellectual Property, Traditional Cultural Expression, and Gender Dimensions of the Benin Bronze Casting Art: An Agenda for Research." In *National Development and Human Security*, edited by F. F. O. Orunmwense. Benin: Uniben Press.

Oriakhogba, D. O., and A. I. Fenemigho. 2014. "Development, Concept and Scope of Copyright Protection in Nigeria: an Overview." *Nnamdi Azikiwe University Journal of International Law and Jurisprudence* 5: 179–191.

Osagie, S. 1985. "The Concept of Material Culture and Contemporary Issues in Nigeria." In *Nigerian Life and Culture*, edited by O. Oyeneye, and Shoremi, 117–138. Ogun State University.

Osei, J. 2006. "The Value of African Taboos for Biodiversity and Sustainable Development". Accessed 29 June 2021. https://jsdafrica.com/Jsda/Fall2006/PDF/Arc_the%20Value%20of%20Arican%20Taboos.pdf.

Owete, K., and J. I. Oviomaigho. 2016. "Culture and Development." In *Culture, Development and Religious Change*, edited by A. O. Kilani, and N. N. Iheanacho, 118. M & J Grand Orbit Communications.

Poorna, R. L., M. Mymoon, and A. Hariharan. 2014. "Preservation and Protection of Traditional Knowledge – Diverse Documentation Initiatives Across the Globe." *Current Science* 107 (8): 1240–1246.

Prompayuk, S., and P. Chairattananon. 2016. "Preservation of Cultural Heritage Community: Cases of Thailand and Developed Countries." *Procedia-Social and Behavioral Sciences* 234: 239–243.

Roy, A. 2008. "Copyright: A Colonial Doctrine in a Post-Colonial Age." *Copyright Reporter* 26 (4): 112.

Sengupta, C. 2001. "Conceptualising Globalisation: Issues and Implications." *Economic and Political Weekly* 36 (33): 3137–3143.

Sithole, J. 2007. "The Challenges Faced by African Libraries and Information Centres in Documenting and Preserving Indigenous Knowledge." *IFLA Journal* 33 (2): 117–122.

Zhang, J. 2017. "Intangible Cultural Heritage and Self-Healing Mechanism in Chinese Culture." *Western Folklore* 76 (2): 197–226.

not been included in the national laws and hence, it is not being implemented in the country. In addition, Nigeria is also not a party to the Nagoya Protocol.

Conclusion

It is imperative for Nigeria to have a Sui Generis system to protect its traditional knowledge from being commercially exploited by other developed countries. It has been mentioned that traditional knowledge cannot be subsumed under any intellectual property regimes but it would be ideal if there is a specific-oriented legislation, which is the sui generis system, to protect indigenous knowledge in Nigeria.

It is therefore important that traditional knowledge be protected and the original custodians of such knowledge be adequately compensated at the same time. Furthermore, it is apt that the community must be protected under indigenous customary laws. As a result of the unique nature of Traditional Knowledge, and to ensure that the law adequately protects the community, the community should also be involved in the whole process of coming up with a *sui generis* regime that will protect their interest.

Notes

1. The Convention on Biological Diversity was at the Earth Summit at the Earth Summit, 1992; Nagoya Protocol on biodiversity was enacted in Japan in 2010.
2. Article 8(j) of the Convention on Biological Diversity 1992.
3. Article 8 (j) of the Convention on Biological Diversity 1992.
4. Article 8(j) Convention on Biological Diversity 1992.
5. United Nations. Traditional Knowledge- An answer to the most pressing global issue. 2019. Accessed through www.un.org>desa>news>social
6. Article 8(j) Convention on Biological Diversity 1992.
7. WIPO Magazine. 2010. What place for customary law in protecting traditional knowledge? Retrieved October 28, 2020 from https://www.wipo.int/wipo.int/wipo_magazine/en/2010_.../
8. The CBD was enacted in 1992.
9. This was developed pursuant to the mandate given at the World Summit on Sustainable Development in 2002 at Johannesburg, South Africa.
10. This was enacted in Nagoya, Japan on October 29, 2010.
11. Article 7, Nagoya Protocol
12. Article 12, Nagoya Protocol
13. Article 15 and 16 of the Protocol, ibid.
14. Nigeria/Country Profile/Access and Benefit-Sharing Clearing ... retrieved from absch.cbd.int> ... >Country Profiles
15. Clearing House mechanism of Nigeria – Home. Retrieved from www.chm.cbd.com.ng
16. WHO has reported that countries in Africa, Asia and Latin America use traditional medicine (TM) to help meet society's primary healthcare needs. In Africa, up to 80% of the population uses TM for healthcare; see WHO Fact Sheet No. 134, revised May 2003. In India, this percentage goes up to 70%.
17. Article 8(j) Convention on Biological Diversity 1992.
18. Article 8(j) Convention on Biological Diversity 1992.

Disclosure statement

No potential conflict of interest was reported by the author(s).

The protection of traditional knowledge under the sui generis regime in Nigeria

Ibijoke P. Byron

ABSTRACT
Africa is a continent that is rich in biodiversity of which Nigeria is not exempted. It depends on the environment for basic survival needs and such knowledge can be used for the provision of food, medicines, cosmetics, to breed better crops, livestock and generally, to shape the ecosystem. There is the danger that biological resources will be depleted which raises concerns on the loss of the habitat and livelihoods of indigenous communities who have nurtured and used these resources for generations. In a bid to ensure that traditional knowledge is preserved, some African countries have taken the urgent step to develop their own specific legislation, which is the *sui generis* legislation. The paper examined the nature of *sui generis* protection under Nigerian law in line with intellectual property rights and customary law. The paper thereby concluded by reiterating that Nigeria, as a matter of urgency, should enact a *sui generis* law.

Introduction

The terminology 'tradition' refers to knowledge systems, expressions of culture, creations and innovations that have been transmitted from one generation to another and such knowledge belongs to a particular people, territory or community. It is necessarily not archaic or static but it evolves in response to a dynamic environment (Dutfield and Suthersanen 2008). In the cultural heritage of any given community, the unique traditions and customs that distinguish them from all other ethnic groups are disclosed. The traditions and customs include agriculture, medicine, environmental practices, language, folklore or art. It is the totality of these practices that include the indigenous knowledge and that is what is passed down from generation to generation (Anyaoku, Nwafor-Onzu, and Aneh 2015). Therefore, what can be described as traditional knowledge includes the historic aspect of any community and their general way of life and practices. Examples of traditional medicinal practices include Indian Ayurvedic medicine, traditional farming practices, knowledge relating to the use of certain biological or chemical resources, traditional dances, songs and rituals (Hassan and Diepeveen 2010).

There is however no effective international legal protection for traditional knowledge and this has led to the proposal for a sui generis system to protect such knowledge.

Another reason why there is the urgent call for the protection of indigenous knowledge is as a result of biopiracy which is characterised by taking without authorisation, the natural resources of a community (Janewa and Tutu 2011). This has been of great concern to the indigenous owner of traditional knowledge. The two international treaties that prevent biopiracy are the Convention on Biological Diversity (CBD) and the Nagoya Protocol on biodiversity.[1]

Traditional knowledge (TK) plays a primary role in supporting sustainable development practices, and protecting the interests of a particular community (Phillips 2016). It refers to innovative knowledge and systems which have evolved in a traditional way and is usually among particular tribes or groups of people sharing the same boundaries, between families, beliefs and culture (Oyewunmi 2015). Traditional knowledge has to do with the preservation of the community involving agriculture, biodiversity and medicinal-related knowledge used to farm, the use of plants, seeds and produce which is utilised to address the health needs of the community (Oyewunmi 2015). There is the growing awareness that such contributions by the community can lead to scientific advancement and technological change (Sinjela and Ramcharan 2005). Worldwide, there are an estimated 300 million indigenous people who have retained social, cultural, economic and political characteristics that are distinct from those of the dominant groups in their respective societies and such persons have fought for the recognition of such rights both nationally and internationally (Sinjela and Ramcharan 2005).

In the last 20 years, traditional knowledge has been the subject of debates and has been described as a cumulative, collective body of knowledge, experience and values held by societies with a history of subsistence in matters relating to land and resource management (Zamparo 1996; Berkes, Colding, and Folke 2000; Ellis 2005). There have however been concerns over the despoliation of the rich biological resources and traditional knowledge of resource-rich countries such as Nigeria for commercial purposes by multinational corporations (Oyewunmi 2015).

The protection of traditional knowledge under intellectual property rights has received attention since the adoption of the CBD in 1992 (Carrea 2001). There is the need to understand the importance and scope of traditional knowledge which includes its widespread use in traditional medicine and farming. The possible forms of protection should then be clarified and why it is important to protect traditional knowledge. Presently, Nigeria does not protect its traditional and indigenous knowledge and as a result of that, there is no effective *sui generis* system. The paper will examine the nature of sui generis protection under the Nigerian law, taking into cognisance the indigenous customary law rites. In addition, the paper will also discuss whether intellectual property rights can protect traditional knowledge.

Importance of traditional knowledge

Traditional Knowledge is a term that is not easy to define and hence, there is no absolute definition. Scholars have therefore described traditional knowledge in several ways. It has been described as a body of knowledge built by a group of people through generations living in close contact with nature which includes a system of classification, a set of empirical observations about the local environment and a system of self-management that governs resource use (Johnson 1992). The CBD defined TK as the knowledge, innovations and practices of indigenous and local communities embodying traditional lifestyles.[2] To further elucidate on the provision, it states that the traditional practices and lifestyles relevant for the conservation and sustainable use of biological diversity should be respected, preserved and maintained by the holders of such innovative knowledge and to encourage the equitable sharing of the benefits arising from the utilisation of such practices.[3]

Traditional knowledge can also be referred to as indigenous knowledge which constitutes part of the cultural and economic wealth of developed and developing countries (Wendland 2002). Moreover, it is a central component for the daily lives of millions of people in developing countries (Carrea 2001) which is the knowledge and practice of indigenous local indigenous communities that have been developed and curated through intergenerational experience with the environment, and shared orally with each generation (Kamau 2009).

Traditional knowledge may be classified into agriculture, ecological, scientific, medicinal and medicinal remedies, knowledge relating to biodiversity, cultural expressions that are traditional which can be in music, dance, artwork designs and the element of language (Visser 2004).

In the global economy, traditional knowledge plays a vital role as traditional communities are responsible for discovering, developing and preserving a tremendous range of medicinal plants, health-giving herbal formulations, agricultural and forest products traded internationally, which may generate economic value (Dutfield 2001). It cuts across numerous issues that include food and agriculture, biodiversity, desertification and the environment, human rights, cultural diversity, trade and economic development (Okujagu 2009). A basic feature of traditional medicine knowledge is that the mode of transmission is oral and it is unwritten but it is passed from one generation to another and is embedded in the practices and experiences of the holder (Gideon Emcee Christian 2009).

TK includes knowledge about the uses, properties and sustainable management of diverse resources that are biological, for instance, traditional crops, medicinal plants, etc. It also forms the basis of the identity of a given cultural identity, contributing to social cohesiveness and thereby reducing vulnerability and poverty (Swiderska 2004). Furthermore, traditional knowledge (TK) is vital for life in a natural environment as it can be of benefit to health, food security and agriculture (Swiderska 2004). For example, traditional farmers have domesticated most of the world's food crops and are continually experimenting to improve their crops and the end result is that there are millions of farmers' varieties that are regarded as the product and embodiment of traditional knowledge (Swiderska 2004). Traditional production and innovation systems provide a wealth of resources and knowledge not only for communities, but for food, agriculture and health needs of the world as a whole (Swiderska 2004). Traditional knowledge expresses the mode by which individuals or communities identify and improve genetic resources over time, which includes processes related to their extraction from nature and its preparation for human usage (Cattier and Panizzon 2004).

The livelihoods of indigenous peoples and the conservation of biodiversity worldwide depend on conserving and protecting traditional knowledge of the use and, of biological and natural resources (Swiderska 2004). This traditional knowledge (TK) has helped develop the millions of farmers' food crop varieties in use today, as well as a wealth of traditional medicines and techniques for sustainable agriculture and resource use and it is the total of these cultural practices that make up the indigenous community (Anyaoku, Nwafor-Onzu, and Aneh 2015). Yet this knowledge is rapidly disappearing due to the increasing threat from both intellectual property regimes and economic globalisation processes that undermine traditional rural livelihoods (Swiderska). This loss is occurring even though the CBD requires member countries to respect, preserve and maintain traditional knowledge, innovations and practices and encourage the fair and equitable- sharing of benefits from their use.[4] International and national policies have so far proved inadequate to protect traditional knowledge. The dominant paradigms of access and benefit-sharing and intellectual property rights have failed to adequately protect TK because they reflect western norms and laws, and focus on protecting intellectual rights (Swiderska 2004).

Traditional knowledge is at the core of the rights of indigenous persons. It is pertinent to state that centuries of history of discrimination, exploitation, dispossession and colonisation have led to the loss of traditional knowledge.[5] Commercial products such as pharmaceutical drugs, cosmetics, crop protection products and seeds are screened from the traditional knowledge of a particular community which involves different species of plants (Swiderska 2004). These crop varieties may be used to develop new commercial crops. Often times, pharmaceutical companies and scientists in developed countries are termed as the commercial users and what is done, is usually to exploit the indigenous knowledge of a particular community and seek intellectual property rights over such knowledge (Swiderska 2004).

Biopiracy and the protection of traditional knowledge

It has been stated that TK and biodiversity are interrelated (Van Overwalle 2005). Prior to TRIPs and CBD, biopiracy was not an issue as medicinal plants were classified as free resources which could be taken out, used and appropriated without any restriction (Fowler and Mooney 1990). However, due to the pillaging of natural resources, developing countries and TK holders were concerned at the instance of biopiracy and wanted a global change and solution for the same. The narratives of appropriation and biopiracy focused on what was perceived as unjust use of genetic resources and traditional knowledge in sectors such as food, medicine and the harm done to the interests of developing nations and communities (Chen 2006)

As a result of the proliferation of the resources of indigenous communities, there have been urgent concern about biopiracy in recent years (Chen 2006, 1). Biopiracy is the unauthorised commercial use of the resources screened from such communities and the patenting of the same without any compensation to the community of origin (Swiderska 2004). In other words, biopiracy is the stealing of the traditional knowledge that has been passed down from generation to generation and the use of products without the authorisation or permission for commercial purposes or the appropriation of traditional knowledge without acknowledging the source of the resources or not paying any compensation to the owners of the bio-cultural knowledge[6] (Coombe 2001; Roht-Arriaza 1996). Hence, affluent companies come from all over the world to visit indigenous peoples in search of intellectual property and to steal their cultural heritage, and this is easy as the world is digitally inclined. It is not a matter of stealing what they have but any community member of the community can be recorded on the video or any sound device that can later be transformed into a digital rendition for access on local or global networks; or it could be easily documented and scientifically practised (Sullivan 2002). In other words, it can also refer to the uncompensated commercial use of biological resources from traditional communities or it could be the patenting of spurious inventions based on such knowledge or resources (Swiderska 2004).

The indigenous people's traditional ownership of such knowledge is not recognised and is therefore deprived of any share or compensation that may have accrued from such practices. The communities thereby lose monetary compensation which could have been garnered from the economic and cultural use and preservation of such knowledge in the local communities (Waziri and Folasasde 2014). Where such knowledge of the communities has been proliferated, it leaves a huge dent in the natural resources conserving the practices and it has the potential of eroding the rich biodiversity of such community (Waziri and Folasasde 2014).

Local and indigenous communities are concerned that the global interest in TK and traditional cultural expressions are not given due respect for the customs, laws and beliefs which have over the years, identified, sustained and shaped the cultural heritage of those communities and which now, appeals to foreigners and such foreigners are not bound by the cultural expressions of the community (Anthony Taubman 2005). Initiatives to safeguard TK, for instance through documenting and publishing, may in fact amount to a betrayal of sacred or social duties to protect their heritage, to the detriment of customary means of preserving and passing on TK. It may amount to an unwanted transfer of treasured knowledge to the public domain, or to passing it on to external interests who are not bound by the traditions embedded in the knowledge that define its spiritual and ethical context (Anthony Taubman 2005).

However, it may be difficult to prevent biopiracy simply because laws required to enforce the provisions in the CBD are absent in countries that provide the knowledge and Intellectual Property Rights regimes allow the patenting of such resources without requiring benefit-sharing. It shows that both the CBD and Intellectual Property Rights are in conflict with each other which makes it difficult in fighting against biopiracy (Swiderska, 5).

Traditional knowledge and customary law

Customary law refers to the laws, customs and practices of local and indigenous and local communities who are close-knitted and which forms the central part of the way of life of such communities. They are entrenched in culture and govern acceptable standards of behaviour that are enforced by members of the community.[7]

Indigenous communities have reiterated that TK protection must be in accordance with customary laws and practices which dictates and governs all aspects of life and have become universally accepted through continuous practice and are applied by traditional authorities (Swiderska 2004).

International laws protecting traditional knowledge

After much agitation from custodians of traditional knowledge, World Intellectual Property Organisation (WIPO) put in place the Intergovernmental Committee on Intellectual

Property, Genetic Resources, Traditional Knowledge and Folklore in order to adopt an international framework for the regulation of such rights (Oyewunmi 2015). There are however other conventions that have been put in place for the protection of TK. Examples are the CBD,[8] the Johannesburg Plan of Implementation,[9] and the Nagoya Protocol to the CBD on Access and Benefit-sharing.[10] These treaties mandate member countries to take legislative, administrative or policy measures to ensure that the benefits arising from the utilisation of traditional knowledge associated with genetic resources are shared in a fair and equitable manner with the owners of such knowledge (Oyewunmi 2015).

The Nagoya protocol ensures that traditional knowledge is accessed with the prior and informed consent and involvement of relevant indigenous and local communities who are the original owners of such right.[11] It also takes into perspective indigenous and local communities' customary laws, community protocols and procedures regarding traditional knowledge associated with genetic resources.[12] Member countries are thereby required to take appropriate legislative, administrative or policy measures to ensure that genetic resources and associated traditional knowledge utilised within their jurisdiction have followed due process by informed consent from the community members and mutually agreed terms have been established based on benefit-sharing legislation or regulatory requirements of the other party.[13] Nigeria is not a party to the Nagoya protocol[14] but is a party to the Convention on Biodiversity became a member to CBD during the Earth Summit in Rio Janeiro in 1992.[15]

There is the need to urgently preserve and protect TK from biopiracy because it is mostly unwritten and is thereby vulnerable to being poached by people simply because they want to acquire intellectual property rights over the knowledge and deny access to the original custodians of the knowledge. The situation is not helped by the fact that intellectual property laws promote uninvited appropriation of the proceeds from TK with no obligation to allow the original owners to have a share in the proceeds of the sale (Waziri and Folasasde 2014). It is now a well-documented fact that TK plays an important role in the global economy and is valuable not only to those who depend on it in their daily lives but also to modern industry and agriculture, (Campbell and Luckert 2002) as most traditional societies depend on this knowledge for their basic necessities.[16]

TK has the potential of being translated into commercial benefits by providing valuable leads for the development of useful products and processes. The valuable leads provided by TK save time, money and investment of modem biotech firms into any research and product development. It is estimated that a hit-rate of 80% or more can be achieved in developing medical drugs where the screening of plants is limited to species used by indigenous communities (Sheldon and Balick 1997).

The issue of protection and preservation of TK at the international level has been brought to the fore at the instance of developing countries because of different concerns and perspectives. A large number of countries rich in genetic resources (GRs) and TK and folklore believe that the traditional communities have been deprived of the benefits from the use of their knowledge, innovations and practices which have been monopolised and used by others, mainly by major companies, without their authorisation and without acknowledging or rewarding them for their knowledge (Verma 2005).

The preponderance of Western culture over indigenous peoples' culture is a fact established since the beginning of the colonisation process. Virtually in every corner of the world, indigenous peoples have gone through a process of assimilation, in which their cultures have been endangered or simply annihilated. However, recently, there has been a growing concern and interest in indigenous and traditional peoples' knowledge especially as it relates to biodiversity, traditional knowledge has become commercially attractive (Greaves 1996). Even though traditional knowledge has been commercially attractive, its use in relation to the effectiveness of screening plants for medical materials has increased to a high percentage (Shiva 2001).

Meanwhile, the livelihoods of indigenous peoples worldwide and the conservation of biodiversity depend on the preservation and protection of TK. Indigenous peoples and rural communities have developed an intimate knowledge of the use and functioning of biological and natural resources over centuries of close dependence on these resources. This TK is vital for life, health, food security and agriculture. It also forms the basis of cultural identity, contributing to social cohesiveness and thereby reducing vulnerability and poverty. Without the strong backing of government policies and/or laws protecting TK, indigenous people possessing this knowledge do not have the capacity to pursue the recognition of their knowledge or to challenge acts of appropriation of their existing knowledge by others (Waziri and Folasasde 2014). This ends up being a great loss not just to the people, but to the economy of the country from which the TK is derived.

There are many reasons why it is important to protect TK because it adds immense value to developing nations which makes it one of the resources that poor people rely on (Liebl and Roy 2004). Misappropriating TK amounts to unduly benefitting from others' knowledge without acknowledging the source or paying appropriate compensation (Cahill 2001). The justification for the protection of traditional knowledge has been expressed in its economic value and the importance of protecting and preventing biopiracy in order to improve the lives of the community members (Waziri and Folasasde 2014).

Efforts have been made in Africa to ensure the Traditional Knowledge is protected against those persons who will misappropriate such resources by putting in place a regional framework. The first was a Model Law for the Protection of the Rights of Local Communities, Farmers and Breeders and for the Regulation of Access to Biological Resources which was an initiative of the then, Organisation of African Unity, which is now known as the African Union (Oyewunmi 2015). There was also the Swakopmund Protocol which also ensured the protection of traditional knowledge and it was adopted under the African Regional Intellectual Property Organisation (ARIPO) (Oyewunmi 2015, at p. 353).

Sui generis regime on the protection of traditional knowledge

The World Intellectual Property Organization has observed that in attempting to tackle the protection of indigenous knowledge through intellectual property rights such as copyrights, patents, plant varieties and trademarks, it may be difficult to protect traditional knowledge through IPRs. This is due to challenges putting traditional knowledge into one-size-fits-all notion such as originality, duration, inventiveness, etc. (Kuruk 1999). In other words, it may not be possible to straight-jacket traditional knowledge under intellectual law branches since it belongs to a particular community at any given time. That is, one person cannot own TK, the entire community must own it. The need for a sui generis system has been recognised and the reason for this alternative to modern intellectual property rights is the argument that IPRs are inadequate to accommodate the interests of TK community holders. However, countries such as India, Philippines and Peru have passed laws to protect TK and establish *sui generis* laws (Carrea 2001).

It has also been held that IPRs are not suitable for indigenous knowledge because the focus is on individuals rather than group rights and protection is offered for a fixed and definite period unlike the indeterminate periods applicable to indigenous knowledge (Carrea 2001, at pgs. 794, 795 and 798). Hence, traditional knowledge does not lend itself to protection using existing legal regimes because it is based on the concept of community property ownership (Wekesa 2006). In other words, TK has been said not to fit in a straight-jacket of IPRs because it is knowledge owned largely by the community and there is no inventor. A limitation of Patent that is in relation to TK, is the requirement of novelty, inventiveness and the commercial viability (Wekesa 2006). A patent is given for an invention that fulfils all three tests namely: the requirements of newness, inventive activity and capability of industrial application.[17] On the other hand, TK does not pass the tests because the knowledge under it is not new, has no inventive step, and the restriction of ownership within communities does not make it commercially viable (Wekesa 2006).

Sui-generis system is the modification of some of the features of intellectual property system so as to properly accommodate the special characteristics of its subject matter (traditional Knowledge) and the specific policy needs which led to the establishment of a different system. In an effort to extend protection to traditional knowledge, various countries have adopted existing intellectual property system to the needs of traditional knowledge holders through sui-generis measures.

Notwithstanding however, the enactment of a sui generis regime poses a number of issues which are complex and it includes the definition of the subject matter of protection, requirements of protection, extent of the rights to be protected, the question of who owns the TK will also arise, then, duration and enforcement measures (Carrea 2001). It is pertinent to note that no internationally binding sui generis regime exists, although there are other regional and national instruments that have been developed in order to assist national governments in complying with their obligations under the Convention for Biological Diversity (Kuruk 2007).

Nonetheless, it is clear that there is a need to recognise traditional knowledge at the international level and also that members of such knowledge owners must be identified within the community (Gopalakrishnan 2002).[18]

Nigeria and traditional knowledge

Nigeria as a nation stands to benefit immensely from the protection of its TK, as it promises to contribute to the economy, as evident in the case of India and other countries that have taken giant strides in the protection of their TK from biopiracy. There is a need for a Sui generis law in Nigeria as the protection of traditional knowledge is considered essential and the enactment of a comprehensive legislation to protect different forms of knowledge is the only way to prevent unauthorised exploitation, particularly by foreign firms for commercial gain. The enactment of a law that is adequately defined will go a long way in ensuring that traditional knowledge is protected.

Nigeria is a signatory to a number of conventions. One of which is the CBD, which was signed in a bid to protect the interests of indigenous communities. The Convention has

References

Anyaoku, Ebele N., Obianuju E. Nwafor-Onzu, and Ebere A. Aneh. 2015. "Collection and Preservation of Traditional Medical Knowledge: Roles for Medical Libraries in Nigeria." *Journal of Library and Indormation Sciences*. 3 (1): 33–43.

Berkes, J., J. Colding, and C. Folke. 2000. "Rediscovery of Traditional Ecological Knowledge as Adaptive Management." *Ecological Applications* 10 (5): 1251–1262.

Cahill, L. S. 2001. "Genetics, Commodifications and Social Justice in the Globalization Era" *Kennedy Institute of Ethics Journal* 11 (3): 221–238.

Campbell, B. M., and M. K. Luckert. 2002. *Uncovering the Hidden Harvest: Valuation Methods for Woodland and Forest Resources*. London: Earthson.

Carrea, C. M. 2001. *Traditional Knowledge and Intellectual Property: Issues and Options Surrounding the Protection of Traditional Knowledge: A Discussion Paper*. Geneva: Quaker United Nations Office.

Cattier, T., and Marion Panizzon. 2004. "Legal Perspectives on Traditional Knowledge: The Case for Intellectual Property Protection." *Journal of International Economic Law* 7 (2): 271–400.

Chen, J. 2006. "There's no Such Thing as Biopiracy ... And It's a Good Thing Too." *McGeorge Law Review* 37: 1.

Christian, G. E. 2009. *Digitization, Intellectual Property and Access to Traditional Medicine Knowledge in Developing Countries – The Nigerian Experience*. Ottawa, Canada: A Research Paper prepared for International Development Research Centre (IDRC).

Dutfield, G. 2001. "TRIPS-Related Aspects of Traditional Knowledge." *Case Western Reserve Journal of International Law* 33: 233.

Dutfield, G., and Uma Suthersanen. 2008. *Global Intellectual Property Law*. Tucson, Arizona: Edward Elgar.

Ellis, Stephen. 2005. "Meaning Consideration?" *A Review of Traditional Knowledge in Environmental Decision Making* 58 (1): 66–77.

Fowler, C., and P. Mooney. 1990. *Shattering: Food, Politics and the Loss of Genetic Diversity*. Arizona: University of Arizona Press.

Gopalakrishnan, N. S. 2002. "Protection of Traditional Knowledge: The Need for a Sui Generis Law in India." *J. World Intellectual Property* 5: 725.

Greaves, T. 1996. "Tribal Rights, in Valuing Local Knowledge: Indigenous People and Intellectual Property 25." (Stephen B. Brush, eds., Island Press).

Hassan, E. Ohid Yaqub, and Stephanie Diepeveen. 2010. "Intellectual Property and Developing Countries: A Review of the Literature." 39–40 (2010).

Janewa, J., and Osei Tutu. 2011. "Emerging Scholars Series: A Sui Generis Regime for Traditional Knowledge: The Cultural Divide in Intellectual Property Law." *15 Intellectual Property Law Review* 147. http://scholarship.law.marquette.edu/iplr/vol15/.

Johnson, M. 1992. "Research on Traditional Environmental Knowledge: Its Development and its Role, in LORE: Capturing Traditional Environmental Knowledge" 3, 4 (Martha Johnson ed.).

Kamau, E. 2009. "Protecting TK Amid Disseminated Knowledge: A New Task for ABS Regimes? A Kenyan Legal View." In *Genetic Resources, Traditional Knowledge and the Law: Solutions for Access and Benefit Sharing*, edited by Evanson Kamau and Gerd Winter, 143–170. Earthscan: London.

Kuruk, P. 1999. "Protecting Folklore under Modern Intellectual Property Regimes: A Reappraisal of the Tensions Between Individual and Communal Rights in Africa and the United States", 48 AM. U.L. Rev. 769, 793.

Kuruk, P. 2007. "The Role of Customary Law Under Sui Generis Frameworks of Intellectual Property Rights in Traditional and Indigenous Knowledge." *Indiana International & Comparative Law Review* 17 (1): 67–118.

Liebl, M., and Tirthankar Roy. 2004. "Handmade in India: Traditional Craft Skills in a Changing World." In *Poor People's Knowledge: Promoting Intellectual Property in Developing Countries*, edited by J. M. Finger and P. Schuler, 53–73. Washington DC: The World Bank and Oxford University Press.

Okujagu, T. F. 2009. *Protecting Traditional Knowledge and Biological Resources in Nigeria: The NNMDA Experience. A Paper Presentation in a Workshop Organized by the Centre for Indigenous Knowledge and Development (CIKAD)*. Ibadan city: University of Ibadan.

Oyewunmi, A. O. 2015. *Nigerian Law of Intellectual Property*. Lagos, Nigeria: University of Lagos Press and Bookshop. p. 349.

Phillips, F. K. 2016. "Intellectual Property Rights in Traditional Knowledge: Enabler of Sustainable Development." *Utrecht Journal of International and European Law* 32 (83): 1–18. https://www.utrechtjournal.org/articles/10.53.

R Coombe. 2001. "The Recognition of Indigenous Peoples' and Community Traditional Knowledge in International Law. 2001." *St. Thomas Law Review* 14: 285. I Mgbeoji Global Biopiracy: Patents, Plants, and Indigenous Peoples. Vancouver: UBC Press 2005.

Roht-Arriaza, Naomi. 1996. "Of Seeds and Shamans: The Appropriation of the Scientific and Technical Knowledge of Indigenous and Local Communities." *Michigan Journal of International Law* 17: 919.

Sheldon, J. W., M. J. Balick, and S. A. Laird. 1997. *Medicinal Plants: Can Utilization and Conservation Co-exist!* 12 Advances in Economic Botany, pp. 1–104.

Shiva, V. 2001. *The Politics of Knowledge at the CBD 2003*. Third World Network. https://twn.my>title>cbd-cn.

Sinjela, M., and R. Ramcharan. 2005. "Protecting Traditional Knowledge and Traditional Medicines of Indigenous Peoples Through Intellectual Property Rights: Issues, Challenges and Strategies." *International Journal on Minority and Group Rights* 12: 1–24.

Sullivan, R. 2002. "Indigenous Cultural and Intellectual Property Rights." *Digital Library Magazine* 8: 5.

Swiderska, K. 2004. "Traditional Knowledge Protection and Recognition of Customary Law: Policy Issues and Challenges. Background Paper for the Planning Workshop on @Protecting community rights over traditional knowledge: Implications of customary laws and practices", London 4–5, 2004.

Taubman, A. 2005. "Saving the Village: Conserving Jurisprudential Diversity in the International Protection of Traditional Knowledge." In *International Public Goods and Transfer of Technology Under a Globalised Intellectual Property Regime*, edited by Keith E. Maskus and Jerome H. Reichman, 521–564. Cambridge: Cambridge University Press.

Van Overwalle, G. 2005. "Protecting and Sharing Biodiversity and Traditional Knowledge: Holder and Use Tools." *Economical ECON* 53: 585.

Verma, S. K. 2005. "Protecting Traditional Knowledge: Is a Sui Generis System an Answer?" *The Journal of World Intellectual Property* 7 (6): 765–805.

Visser, C. J. 2004. "Making Intellectual Property Laws Work for Traditional Knowledge." In *Poor People's Knowledge, Promoting Intellectual Property*, edited by Finger Schuler, 207–234. A co-publication of the World Bank and Oxford University Press.

Waziri, K., and Awomolo Omatayo Folasasde. 2014. "Protection of Traditional Knowledge in Nigeria: Breaking the Barriers." *Journal of Law, Policy and Globalization* 29: 1–12.

Wekesa, Moni. 2006. "What is *Sui Generis* system of Intellectual Property Protection?" African Technology Policy Studies Network. http://repository.daystar.ac.ke/xmlui/handle/1234.

Wendland, W. 2002. "'Intellectual Property, Traditional Knowledge and Folklore: WIPO's Exploratory Program' II, Max-Planck Institute for Foreign and International Patent." *Copyright and Competition Law* 33: 485–504.

Zamparo, J. 1996. "Informing the Fact: Inuit Traditional Knowledge Contributes Another Perspective." *Geoscience Canada* 23 (4): 261–266.

The digital tax reform for Africa: customised or one-size-fits-all approach?

Nikolai Milogolov and Azamat Berberov

ABSTRACT
We employ analytical, case study and economic analysis approaches to explore trends and potential outcomes of tax policy reforms addressing challenges of digital business transformation in Africa. We find the striking level of differences among the twenty-six examined African countries, in both their positions in global and regional economy, and in digital capacities of states and their tax administrations. The potential outcome of the discussion of multilateral reform at the Organisation for Economic Cooperation and Development (OECD) global governance level and unilateral reforms such as digital services taxes and its implications for African states are discussed in this context. Tax policy proposals are suggested for delineated groups of African states based on the idea of narrowly targeted digitally related policy for the leaders and broad cooperation between all the African states. Such an approach can ensure the economic potential of multilateral cooperation among developing countries and defend their economic and fiscal interests at the global tax governance level.

Introduction

We can observe today the very intense ongoing global tax governance discussion, which is moderated by the OECD,[1] about the future of corporate income tax rules in relation to taxation of the global profits of the major highly digitalised businesses, primarily internet search engines, e-commerce platforms and social networks (OECD Pillar 1 Proposal). At the core of the discussion are the issues of attributing a larger share of taxable profits of such businesses to the market countries based on the argument that users of the digital products whose data is collected and exploited by such businesses are physically located in these countries. Such users can be regarded as input resources in the value-creation chain of the digitalised businesses; therefore, virtual interaction with these users is regarded as creation of the virtual marketing asset in the market country.

The global discussion also deals with the technical design of the reform and a choice between multilateral 'global consensus' solution proposed by the OECD and unilateral solutions such as digital services taxes (DST) introduced in many countries unilaterally.

As different countries have different economic preconditions and trends in digital business transformation, such differences between countries are reflected in their attitudes towards the OECD Pillar 1 Proposal. For example, the United States is a home economy for the largest digitalised multinational enterprises (MNE) (Google, Apple, Amazon, Facebook, etc.) and therefore is not interested in sacrificing its tax revenues from taxing their foreign profits to market countries (Martin 2019). Another position is typical for the largest European countries, which are the largest market for the US-based digital businesses. For example, France, Italy and the United Kingdom are claiming their rights to tax the income of digitalised businesses based on the argument of the significant economic contribution of the well-off populations of these developed countries into the profits obtained by the US-based digitalised businesses are obtained from virtually engaging with users from these countries (Leigh 2020).

This discussion is relevant for Africa, as the digitalisation has a strong impact on the economies, business practices and societies of African countries, so officials from African countries must have their positions regarding the future of tax rules (Monkam et al. 2019). However, as suggested in this article, based on the analysis of the economic indicators for the selected African countries, the situation is not so black-and-white regarding potential positions of African states towards the discussed ideas, such as Pillar 1, DST and related corporate tax developments. The main reason for this is the inherent difference between African countries, which cannot be ignored in the context of digital transformation. Such differences are especially striking in an area such as the role of individual African countries in the modern global capitalist economy, which is dominated by the MNEs' activity. Other important differentiating factors are the level of penetration of digital technologies in the individual African economies and the level of modernity and efficiency of their tax revenue authorities.

In this research, we are sorting the African countries into several groups based on an analysis of indexes illustrating the mentioned differences between the analysed states. We are then suggesting several design proposals of tax reform most fit for the different groups of African countries based on their inherent economic preconditions. These proposals can potentially be used by the tax policy makers as starting reference points in the discussion of the design of the reforms and for their national position towards taxing the digitalised businesses during international tax governance discussions at global and regional levels.

Research is structured as follows: in the first section, we formulate the goal of the research and general research agenda and context; in the second section, we describe our research approach; in third section, we present the results of the analysis of economic indicators and the results of groupings based on indexes; in the fourth section, we discuss the arguments around different tax policy options; in the fifth section, we discuss current trends in domestic tax policy and in digital business in the individual African countries belonging to different groups and in the sixth section, we formulate high-level tax policy proposals.

Research approach

The aim of this research is to formulate high-level international tax policy recommendations based on the analysis of the economic significance of African economies for MNEs. Such recommendations also account for the level of digitalisation, efficiency of tax administration, digital business developments in Africa and specific features of the possible tax reforms addressing challenges of international digitalisation in the context of international competition and coordination.

The milestone of this research is the analysis of indicators resulting in groupings of the examined African states, which is presented in the third section and discussed in detail here. However, the country groupings is only one of the three inputs that we subsequently use for the fulfilment of the final goal of this research. Other inputs are the results of the analysis of risks and possibilities of different tax policy reform options in the context of African economies (which is presented in the fourth section) and the results of the analysis of the existing international tax policy and digital business developments in the individual African states belonging to the different groups (presented in the fifth section). We use analytical review and case study approach to summarise tax policy arguments and delineate the related developments and reforms in individual African states. Tax policy recommendations based on the results presented in the third to fifth sections are formulated in the, concluding, sixth section. This is summarised in Table 1.

We employ the following 4-step methodology for the grouping of African countries:

1. We compose the indicators based on collected data for the large sample of 26 African economies for which comparable high-quality data is available;
2. We perform a comparative analysis of these 26 African countries based on the construction of two composite indicators (indexes) showing (a) the significance of each country's economy for international foreign direct investments (FDI) and MNEs' activity and (b) the level of national digital readiness and tax administration development;
3. We group the countries into the three groups based on the results of the comparative analysis of these indexes, which is based on the relative differences between the analysed countries;
4. We analyse the composition of groups for anomalies and consider regrouping or the creation of more groups if this is necessary.

The details of calculations made at three steps of analysis are described in Tables 2–4.

As explained in Table 2, we obtain eight different indicators (a–h) for our sample of countries resulting from Step 1. We use these indicators for our comparative analysis. We account them with the different weights in order to construct two composite indicators (indexes) showing (a) the significance of each country's economy for international

Table 1. Summary of the overall research approach.

Input	(1) Results of the country grouping based on the indexes showing their potential role in the digitalised cross-border business in the context of tax administration
	(2) Discussion of main tax policy options: unilateral solution (DST) vs. coordinated solution (Pillar 1)
	(3) Discussion of tax policy and digital business developments in the individual African countries
Output	High-level tax policy recommendations for different groups of countries based on the results of the analysis

Source: authors.

Table 2. Details of data collection and construction of indicators.

Step 1 – Data collection and construction of author's indicators	
Input	Data for 26 African countries for their: *(a) GDP size (Gross domestic product 2019); (b) FDI inward and outward stocks (UNCTAD 2020); (c) charges for the use of intellectual property, receipts and payments (World Bank Open Data 2020a, 2020b); (d) country ranking in Paying Taxes PricewaterhouseCoopers (PwC) Index (Overall ranking and data tables); (e) percentage of the population using the Internet (World Bank Open Data 2020c); (f) country rank in business to consumer (B2C) e-commerce index (UNCTAD 2019).*
Output 1	Authors' calculations of indicators based on the data: (a) *FDI stock balance = (Outward FDI – Inward FDI stock) / GDP;* (b) *Total FDI/GDP ratio = (Outward FDI stock + Inward FDI stock) / GDP;* (c) *GDP relative size = GDP of i-country/GDP of all countries;* (d) *Royalty balance = (Royalties received – Royalties paid) / GDP;* (e) *Net rate of royalty return on FDI = (Royalties received / FDI outward) – (Royalties paid / FDI inward)* (f) *country ranking in Paying Taxes PWC Index (Overall Ranking and data tables) = as given;* (g) *Internet users, as share of population = as given;* (h) *country score in B2C e-commerce UNCTAD index = as given.*
Output 2	We assess the relative difference between the countries in the sample (in %) for each of the indicators in Output 1. To achieve this aim, we: (9) *calculate the medium meaning for the sample of 26 countries;* (10) *assess the level of the relative difference between the actual meaning for individual country and medium meaning for the countries in sample (in given amount) and* (11) *weight the calculated difference by the difference between the minimum and maximum amount in the sample.*

Source: authors.

FDIs & MNEs' activity and (b) the level of national digital readiness and tax administration development. The details of this step are illustrated in Table 3.

As explained in Table 3, we derived two indexes which, in their combination, show the potential role of the individual African states in the emerging digitalised economy in the context of their tax policy. The results are then presented in graphical form in Figure 1, where the dots corresponding to the potential leaders in the digital age among the examined African countries are situated at the upper-right quadrant of the graph. We use the results of Step 2 to explicitly illustrate the differences among countries. However, a stricter approach towards groupings of the states is performed afterwards, based on the level of strength of Indexes A and B for individual countries (low/medium/high). The details of this step are illustrated in Table 4.

As explained in Step 3 in Table 4, we finally derive three groups of countries based on the estimations of the Indexes A and B. In Step 4, we amend these results based on the level of relative differences between the countries. If the results for any country deviate

Table 3. Details of data collection and construction of composite indicators (indexes).

Step 2 – Comparative analysis of indicators	
Input	Indicators a to g, as calculated at Step 1
Output 1A	Constructing composite indictor (Index A) illustrating the significance of country's economy for international FDIs & MNEs' activity: *accounting the first five indicators from Step 1 (from [a] to [e]) with equal weights of 20% each.*
Output 1B	Constructing composite indictor (Index B) illustrating the level of national digital readiness and tax administration development: *accounting the three remaining indicators from Step 1 (from [f] to [h]) with equal weights of 1/3 each.*
Output 2	Graphically (see Figure 1 in the third section) showing the composite indictors (indexes) as calculated for individual African countries: (1) Index A is represented by the x axis; (2) Index B is represented by the y axis.

Source: authors.

Table 4. Details of country grouping based on indexes.

	Step 3 – Country grouping based on indexes
Input	Estimations of Indexes A and B for individual countries as calculated at Step 2
Output 1	We divide the interval of values of Indexes A and B for the sample countries on three equal parts. We then group countries in three groups based on their values separately for their position in Indexes A and B and score them: (1) *high level – country value is in the upper third of the sample (3 scores);* (2) *medium level – country value is in the medium third of the sample (2 scores);* (3) *low level – country value is in the lower third of the sample (1 score).*
Output 2	Country groupings based on the aggregate scoring for the combined results of Output 1 on three groups: (4) *5–6 scores – high/medium economic significance & high/medium digital readiness (at least one index is high);* (5) *4 scores – medium economic significance & digital readiness or combination of high meaning of one indictor with low meaning of another;* (6) *3 scores – medium/low economic significance & digital readiness (at least one index is low).*

Source: author's.

too much from the others in the same group, we consider introducing a separate group for such anomaly countries. The results of applying this methodology for the sample of 26 African countries are presented in Figure 1.

Estimation of indexes of economic significance and domestic digitalisation capabilities for African countries

In Figure 1, we graphically illustrate the results of the comparative analysis for the sample of 26 African countries performed by the authors in line with the methodology described in the second section.

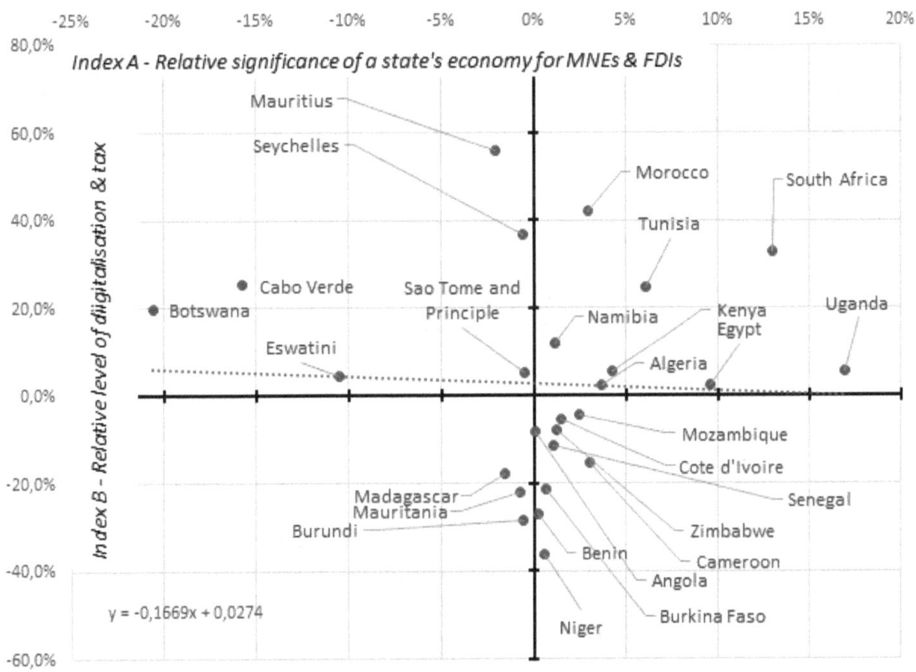

Figure 1. Indexes constructed by authors for the sample of 26 African countries.

We can make three observations resulting from the comparative analysis based on two estimated indexes.

First, as we see in Figure 1, the trend line is sloping slightly downward. This means there is an overall negative trend (or at least an absence of positive relation) between the level of the economic significance of state's economy for international FDI and MNEs' activity (Index A) and the level of digitalisation and tax system development (Index B). This result shows that stronger African economies are not, as a rule, more developed in digitalisation and do not necessarily have more developed tax systems. This can be explained by the fact that digitalisation and developments in tax administration can spread and evolve faster than economic development, so we do not observe the correlation between the two indexes. This observation has an important role in discussing the possible cooperation among African countries in addressing tax challenges of digitalisation. If such cooperation will include all African countries, there will be no large group of strong leaders in terms of both digitalisation and economic potential. Such strong leaders can potentially deviate the outcomes of cooperation in their favour because of the skill-based inequality in tax administration and because of the opposite economic interests.

Second, while it is generally true for the sample of analysed African countries that the level of the digitalisation and the level of tax administration are spread relatively equally between more and less developed countries, there is still a group of leaders (relatively small number of states) and a group of outsiders (relatively large number of states) in both their digital development and economic role. We can especially emphasise the role of South Africa as absolute leader in both economic role and digital developments (the only country with 3 scores for its level of both Indexes A and B), accounting for almost a quarter of the sample countries' GDP. Therefore, we suggest that this country shall be included in a special Group 1, consisting of only one country for the purposes of subsequent analysis in this research, as its indexes deviate too much from the other countries.

Third, African countries significantly differ from one another in both their economic positions (Index A) and their digital readiness and tax administration level (Index B), which can be interpreted as an argument in favour of taking into account these differences when designing tax policy in relation to digitalisation. As such tailored tax policy shall be built around specific countries, we present the result of our grouping in Table 5.

As we can observe from the analyses in Table 5 and Figure 1, we can now group the countries into four groups. The half of the 26 examined states (13 states) belong to Group 4, the group of African countries with the most striking level of underdevelopment, while only seven countries belong to Groups 1 and 2, the groups representing the potential leaders of digital business transformation in the African continent. The remaining six states belong to Group 3, the group of the medium-developed states in the context of our analysis. These countries do not have enough potential to become digital leaders of Africa at the moment; however, they can potentially challenge the digital leadership of the others in the event their development continues in the future.

- Group 1 (6 scores for both Indexes) – the highest level of combined scoring for Indexes A and B in combination with exceptionally high share in the overall African economic activity (GDP and FDIs): South Africa.

Table 5. Results of grouping based on estimated indicators.

		Significance of country's economies for international FDIs & MNE's activity		
		Low	*Medium*	*High*
Digital readiness & tax administration development	*High*	Cabo Verde	Mauritius Morocco Seychelles	South Africa
	Medium	Botswana Eswatini	Algeria Kenya Mozambique Namibia Sao Tome and Principle	Egypt Tunisia Uganda
	Low	No countries	Angola Benin Burkina Faso Burundi Cameroon Cote d'Ivoire Madagascar Mauritania Niger Senegal Zimbabwe	No countries

Source: authors' groupings based on comparative estimations of Indexes A and B.

- Group 2 (5 scores for both Indexes) – high/medium economic significance and high/medium digital readiness (at least one index is high): Egypt, Mauritius, Morocco, Seychelles, Tunisia, Uganda.
- Group 3 (4 scores for both Indexes) – medium economic significance and digital readiness or combination of high meaning of one indictor with low meaning of another: Algeria, Cabo Verde, Kenya, Mozambique, Namibia, Sao Tome and Principle.
- Group 4 (less than 4 scores for both Indexes) – medium/low economic significance and digital readiness (at least one index is low): Angola, Benin, Botswana, Burkina Faso, Burundi, Cameroon, Cote d'Ivoire, Eswatini, Madagascar, Mauritania, Niger, Senegal, Zimbabwe.

These groupings will be used as an input for designing and discussing tailored tax policy recommendations for the delineated groups of African countries in the further sections of this article.

Digital tax reform for Africa in the global tax governance context: international cooperation or competition

Multilateral tax cooperation in the African context

Multilateral cooperation is a relatively rare issue in the international tax treaty context, where a bilateral format still prevails. Multilateral tax cooperation usually has very limited scope, both in terms of covered areas of regulation (such as only indirect taxes or only special types of passive income: dividends, royalties, interests) and in terms of participant countries (such as countries already having strong economic ties). So, the necessary prerequisite for successful international tax coordination is either common economic interests or common aims of the cooperating countries (Broekhuijsen and Vording 2016).

As recent experience of international tax cooperation under the umbrella of the OECD's Base Erosion Profits Shifting Project (BEPS) shows, the role of global economic and political leaders from the developed world (such as the United States and G7 economies) is very important in such global projects (Brauner 2016), however, new leaders from the emerging world also arise, and their conceptual positions find reflections in the deliverables of such global projects. This can be seen, for example, in the update of the OECD Transfer Pricing Guidelines (2017b), partly incorporating the Chinese approach of accounting for location saving advantages when determining transfer pricing (Ainsworth and Shact 2014).

African interests can also be reflected in global tax reforms if their economic power increases or if they collaborate with others in the emerging world in their tax policy positions. Currently, both areas are problematic, as most African states (with the exception of South Africa) do not likely have a well-determined positions for their international tax policy related to digital business, and as the African continent accounts for only 3% of global GDP and 17% of global population (Coleman 2020) while most of the global digital solutions come from either the US or Chinese economies. Therefore, the authors suggest that coordination of international tax policy among African states is a necessary precondition for successful economic policy in the current challenging times; otherwise, African states risk directing their limited administrative capacities into the wrong priorities and missing their most important concerns.

Such cooperation is potentially feasible, and there are already several examples for this, including the African Tax Administration Forum (ATAF) Model Tax Convention (2009) and the ATAF DST Guidelines (2020b). These developments represent soft power recommendations, so their importance can increase, resulting from the network effects and benefits of coordination if these recommendations are followed by the African countries. However, such cooperation can face several obstacles because of the inherent economic and digital development inequality across Africa, as is discussed in the third section.

Distribution of taxing rights between source and residence state in context of digitalisation: Shifting of the existing global paradigm

The key economic foundation on which the distributions of taxing rights between the states are based is the principle of taxation in accordance with the part of the economic value that is created in any state. This value-creation concept was historically understood based on the analysis of the supply value chain, and this was reflected in the provisions of the OECD MC (2017a), UN MC (2018) and OECD TP Guidelines (2017b). However, recently we have been able to observe the shift in the understanding of this concept and articulation of the growing importance of the demand-side arguments as justifying the economic value created in the state where the consumers (or users in the case of digital products) reside. This shift in argumentation reflects the broader economic interests of some emerging and developing economies with large and growing populations. Chinese transfer pricing concept of 'market premium' (Ainsworth and Shact 2014) and the Indian emerging approach of profit attribution to permanent establishments (PE) are two examples of such demand-side developments (International Tax Review 2019).

The economic nature of transactions in a digitalised economy can vary substantially: from business-to-business (B2B) transactions (such as providing rights for the business use of copyrighted software under exclusive licence, supplying cloud computing services or online advertisement) to business-to-consumer (B2C) digitalised services (such as supplying audio-visual content, giving access to free digital products or providing unexclusive licence to use a word processor at home with constant updating) (OECD 2017a). Such economically different transactions are classified differently for the purposes of double tax treaties, based on the amount of rights transferred to the recipient (as either royalties or business income) (OECD 2017a), which leads to different levels of taxation of such income in the source state. In the case of royalties, the source state's taxing rights usually exist but are limited by tax treaties. In the case of business income, the source state does not have rights to tax in cases where no physical presence by a foreign company exists.

Economic consideration in the background of the current distribution of taxing rights between resident and source states is the differentiation between the income (a) earned by the owners as factors of production (such as the physical and financial capital in broad meaning and intellectual property) and (b) earned by the enterprise itself resulting from its own 'usual' business (through the work of its employees). This is mostly reflected in the different treatment of (a) passive income such as dividends, interests, royalties and capital gains and (b) active income such as business profits.

Two straightforward tax policy options for reform in front of African countries include either unilateral or multilateral reform. Both of these reforms result in increasing the level of taxation of business profits of digitalised MNEs at the source states; however, both the mechanics and the consequences of achieving these policy goals are different, as discussed in the following sections.

Unilateral digital reform: pros and cons

Unilateral measures aimed at achieving the goal of ensuring more taxation of digitalised businesses at the source state include either reforming existing corporate income tax concepts (such as permanent establishment) or introducing new DST (UN 2019). The first group of measures has very little, if any, practical effect because even large broadening of domestic corporate income tax (CIT) concepts aimed at taxing foreign enterprise at source are still limited by double tax treaties. However, amending a double tax treaty needs the approval of the foreign parties of such a treaty, which might have an opposite economic interest. A multilateral effort aimed at amending existing double tax treaty architecture is discussed in section 'Multilateral solution: pros and cons'. Therefore, we focus in this subsection on the second option (DST), which in its essence is an indirect tax (like excise tax in its design and mechanics) imposed on turnover of foreign suppliers from supplying digital services based on data collected from the users residing in the source (market) country. Anticipated effects of the DST reform in the context of African states will also be discussed (ATAF 2020a).

Arguments in favour of introducing DST are threefold. First, its simple design and mechanics, which can be especially important in an African context, are characterised by the limited expertise and resources of tax administration. Second, its potential to generate revenue in the current times of urgent fiscal needs and third, the political attractiveness of taxing foreign capital and using the funds for the support of the domestic enterprises and economy. These arguments are especially striking in the current times of the COVID-19 pandemic-driven economic slowdown, and the need for revenues to finance recovery in combination with accelerated digitalisation for the same reasons (Cruz Cano 2020).

However, such a simple solution as DST also has its problems. First, potential double taxation of profits under CIT and DST systems; second, gross basis of taxation resulting in potential inconsistency between the level of taxation at source and the level of economically justified financial result of foreign companies at source market; third, the creation of a potential barrier for the penetration of foreign digitalised solutions and their accessibility for domestic businesses and consumers and fourth, potential confrontation from the developed-world side, which is the leading provider of economic aid to African countries.

Multilateral solution: pros and cons

The Pillar 1 tax policy proposal promoted by OECD is a multilateral solution aimed at introducing new concepts resulting in attributing more profits to market countries to address the challenges of digitalisation. The proposed solution is based around dividing the global profits of the largest global digitalised MNEs into three parts (amounts A, B and C), subject to different rules of profit-sharing between countries (OECD 2019).

The most discussable part of Pillar 1 is the Amount A component, which in fact is a formulary-based simplified solution aimed at delineating part of global tax profits of MNEs and attributing it to market states, even if there is no physical presence of a foreign company in the market state. After discussing this idea in 2019, OECD proposed a mechanism targeted at companies with high levels of digitalisation and virtual engagement with users (such as social networks and internet search engines and platforms), and also consumer-facing businesses, which use digital technologies for the development of their customer base.

The Amount B component is based on the existing transfer pricing methodology and is applied only if there is a physical presence in the state. Amount C is the remaining part of profits, which are allocated in case a dispute arises between the states about the exact amount of Amount A and Amount B. This can be the case when determining the remuneration for marketing and distributional functions. That is why the new Pillar 1 rules promoted by the OECD shall be introduced in combination with the global tax administration and dispute resolution mechanisms.

The basic analysis of risks and opportunities of joining Pillar 1 for African states shall account for its scope, which includes only MNEs with a global turnover of at least 750 million Euro (OECD 2019). As there are currently no such MNEs with headquarters in any African country (Global 500 2020), joining the OECD Pillar 1 proposal will not deteriorate the competitiveness of African business. Therefore, the analysis of pros and cons shall be focused more on fiscal and administrative considerations rather than on considerations of international competitiveness. As mentioned in the literature, Pillar 1 will not eliminate international tax competition for incorporating and locating value-creation functions of MNEs (OECD 2021), because it does not limit the tax policy options for countries to increase the competitiveness of their economies by introducing new tax incentives for research and development (R&D), intellectual property (IP), the relocation of key staff or other highly mobile assets and functions of MNEs (Hufbauer 2020). Therefore, from an economic perspective, African countries can either also enter into such international tax competitions, which can hamper their corporate tax bases, or ensure a level playing field by harmonising their systems in relation to digital business.

Fiscal and administrative arguments for African countries joining the OECD Pillar 1 proposal are built around the following: first, this is an international consensus solution; second, new rules will mostly be administered at the international tax governance level and accompanied with tax administration assistance missions from the OECD and third, joining the initiative will likely increase the tax revenues of African states. However, these straightforward pros of Pillar 1 for the African region are not as convincing as they may seem. Pillar 1 is, in its essence, a hybrid solution, incorporating new formulary apportionment rules and existing transfer pricing methodology; therefore, the tax revenue effect can be very modest or at least relatively lower than under the DST system. Additionally, Pillar 1 limits the potential reforms in African economies, introducing more simple solutions, such as, for example, a simple withholding tax at source on all B2B outbound digital payments, which can be more in line with their fiscal interests and administrative capabilities. The last argument is especially important, considering the limited capacities of local tax administrations in controlling complex transfer pricing transactions inside digitalised MNEs in case some physical presence of such MNEs exist in the African economy.

Current trends in tax policy and digital transformation in Africa

In this section, we present the results of analytical review of current trends in tax reforms in the examined African countries relating to digital transformation, which we consider significant for the purposes of our analysis. We focus in particular on (1) unilateral measures aimed at taxing profits of digitalised MNEs considered or introduced in several African states, (2) the broader context of digital business transformation and specifics of existing international tax methodology in the context of digital business in several countries, which we identified among the leaders (South Africa and Egypt).

Unilateral measures aimed at taxing profits of digitalised MNEs considered or introduced in several African states

The issues of corporate taxation of digitalised businesses are increasingly relevant for Africa, as it has a large and fast-growing population increasingly reliant on telecommunication and digital solutions for overcoming the challenges of development, such as facilitating small business access to financing, consumers and suppliers and curbing the shadow economy (World Bank 2018). However, penetration of foreign digital platforms into the local markets not only has potentially game-changing advantages, it can also lead to exponentially growing fiscal risks arising from the potential inability of taxing income obtained by foreign digital businesses without any physical presence. This challenge is not unique for Africa, however, considering that the speed of digital transformation in some African states and the absence of their own developed industrial base means that fiscal risks are higher for them.

This challenge is closely related to the remaining opportunities for tax base erosion and profit shifting into low-tax jurisdictions through different channels. Numerous African countries joined the OECD/G20-promoted global BEPS Project and other international initiatives aimed at curbing international fiscal evasion and avoidance, however the efficiency of such international cooperation for the African continent is still rather modest (ATAF 2019). A key reason for this is that it takes time for national fiscal authorities to develop capabilities in auditing transfer pricing and other tax planning strategies by MNEs and for tax policymakers to develop an efficient and independent tax treaty strategy.

The importance of the digital fiscal problems could be seen in developing countries (including African states) by the prioritisation of their national positions of the corresponding BEPS Project's Actions (relating to addressing the challenges of digitalisation [Action 1] and to artificial avoidance of permanent establishment status [Action 7]) (UN 2014c). For example, Ghanian representatives mentioned that the taxation of e-commerce requires more attention from international organisations (UN 2014a). Key domestic challenges mentioned by African country delegates include existing impaired and distortive tax legislation and untransparent tax administration practices in relation to foreign MNEs, which can lead to potential corruption and lack of reasonable fiscal control (UN 2014b).

The COVID-19 global pandemic exacerbated digital tax challenges throughout the world, as it stimulated the growth in teleworking and contributed to windfall profits of the largest digital MNEs at a time of global economic slowdown for other businesses. Such growing inequality between the high-end digital MNEs and stagnating local businesses, especially in the service and small business sectors, is also relevant for African tax policy context. The urgency of addressing the issue is stressed by growing fiscal deficits and limited capacities for fiscal manoeuvring by African economies (Moore 2020). The mentioned developments are reflected in tax reform practices in some African states, which are discussed in the following section.

First, some African states are introducing or currently considering DST based on the model and example of European states (Asen 2021). The scope of digital businesses included in DST taxation is different across such African countries; however, general DST design is very similar; taxation of the gross amount of revenue flows derived by the foreign digitalised businesses from supplying digital services at domestic market at relatively low rate (1.5–5%). Summary of developments in three states is presented in Table 6.

The second type of the digital tax reform is reflected in the collaboration of African states with the OECD in the course of continuation of the BEPS Inclusive Framework and joining the multilateral solution for the digital economy. Several African countries acknowledged that joining Pillar 1 can be a more efficient approach than introducing DST unilaterally. Such a position was stated by Senegalese officials (Sarfo 2020). International tax policy discussion in South Africa is rather controversial; experts from Davis Tax Committee stress the advantages and recommend joining the Pillar 1 proposal (Deloitte tax at hand 2020); however, there are also concerns that Pillar 1 will not address the digital-related tax challenges of developing African countries (Businesstech 2020). Egypt's minister of finance stated in 2019 that countries can introduce DST for a limited list of digital services, however, the technical proposal still was not published,

Table 6. DST in African countries.

Country	Rate	Base	Threshold	Effective date
Kenya	1.5%	Income accruing through a 'digital marketplace', being a platform that enables the direct interaction between buyers and sellers of goods and services through electronic means	None	1 January 2021
Tunisia	3%	Gross income from sale of computer applications and digital services	None	1 January 2020
Zimbabwe	5%	Gross income from satellite broadcasting services in respect of the provision or delivery of television or radio programmes, and on e-commerce operators providing or delivering goods or services to persons resident in Zimbabwe	Revenue more than USD500K in any year of assessment	1 January 2019

Source: Deloitte tax at hand (2020).

so it is unclear in what exact design such tax will be introduced (El-Kamel 2019). The slow speed of reforms can be explained by the attempts to maintain good relations at the intentional governance level at the OECD, where there is strong opposition in favour of international consensus and against domestic unilateral digital taxes.

The third kind of reform can be described as the introduction of alternative approaches by some African states. One example of such developments can be seen in Nigeria, which is considering introducing a 'significant digital presence' concept as part of its CIT legislation (Obayemi 2021). Such reform is based on the idea of extending nexus criteria – from a physical to mere virtual economic presence – for foreign company business income to fall into the scope of domestic taxation at source. Such an approach is likely inspired by reforms already introduced in some countries, for example, in India, Slovakia and Israel (Aslam and Shah 2020). The anticipated tax revenue impact of this kind of reform is very modest because its legal effect is still limited by the tax treaties, which are still based on a permanent establishment concept, requiring the physical presence of a foreign company for taxing its income at source. That is why even in Israel and Slovakia, which followed such a reform approach recently, its implementation was faced with compliance and legal problems of treaty override and legal uncertainty. Moreover, Israel is currently considering introducing DST instead (Hoke 2019).

South Africa as capital-exporting country in the digital age

As South Africa is a regional economic and digital leader, its tax policy interests differ from the other examined African states. This country has a positive FDI balance and is interested in increasing the inflow of FDI into its economy, and it, therefore, does not prioritise source taxation in its international tax policy (UNCTAD 2020). While an appropriate level of taxation at source can be achieved by South Africa by joining the OECD Pillar 1 solution, one of its most challenging current international tax policy goals is to ensure the necessary level of taxation of worldwide profits of its resident companies. This policy goal is especially controversial in the digital context, as the concept of corporate residence is erosive in a digitalised reality.

The concept of corporate residence is a central and basic concept in corporate taxation design for the worldwide system of taxation (as in South Africa). Such jurisdictions tax the profits of its residents derived worldwide, both from in state and outside sources. The residence is usually determined by the number of tests showing the personal nexus of a corporate entity with a country, such as its incorporation under domestic corporate law of the country, managing the company from the territory of the country or both. The second test becomes problematic in the digital age, as it is built on the physical nexus of managers with the territory of the country at the time of performing their management functions. However, in times of modern technologies and globalisation, companies can pick and choose their tax residency location for financial-planning purposes (Dagan 2017).

Today, under South Africa's domestic tax law, there are two principal tests of determining corporate tax residence: (1) place of incorporation and (2) place of effective management (POEM) (Van Zyl 2020). In the administrative manuals of South Africa's tax authorities, it is mentioned that POEM is a unique place where the key management and commercial decisions that are necessary for the entrepreneurial team as a whole are made. In other words, POEM requires determining who the people are in company who 'call the shots' and perform 'realistic positive management' on a 'case by case' basis, taking into account all the facts and circumstances such as, for example, the location of the head office of the company housing key management seats and where crucial decisions are made (South African Revenue Service 2015).

So, for example, a digital platform operating taxi-riding services in Cape Town and other capital towns of Africa can be incorporated offshore and managed by international team meetings via virtual Zoom conference calls. In this case, such a company will not be considered South Africa's tax resident. That is why the current approach towards corporate residence can potentially have fiscal risks of base erosion and aggressive tax planning in the context of digital transformation.

Egypt as net importer of intellectual property

Countries of Northern Africa also have a prominent role among the examined African states, and Egypt can be considered one of the leaders in Africa in its digital transformation. As analysts noticed (Fitch Solutions 2018), there are several important comparative advantages of this country, including a high proportion of young population, proactive economic government policy aimed at supporting IT and the population's digital literacy, the growth of e-commerce consumer market (which includes more than 30 million customers and is the largest not only in Africa but also in the Arab world) and time consistency with Europe (which, for example, was one of the key reasons for choosing Egypt as an outsource hub by France Telecom).

Egypt's system of taxing MNEs can be characterised as rather fiscally oriented, with relatively high withholding taxes for taxation of royalties and service fees paid to non-residents, both at the domestic level and at the tax treaty level (Worldwide Tax Summaries Online 2020). Egypt is also a member of the BEPS Inclusive Framework and the most important anti-avoidance rules are present in its domestic tax law and tax administration. Egypt's tax system also includes tax incentives such as special economic zones, possibilities to reduce withholding taxes for interest and dividends and other provisions aimed at attracting foreign capital (OECD 2020). Therefore, we suggest that in the medium-term prospective, Egypt's corporate income tax system does not require dramatic reforms. However, in our opinion, several reforms aimed at increasing its competitiveness can ensure its consistent leadership in the digital age among African states.

We suggest reforming mechanisms of taxing royalties paid to non-residents, as these payments are crucial and are included in the cost of intellectual property transferred by foreign MNEs to their subsidiaries in Egypt. Current mechanism of taxing royalties at source can be described as simple and also protectionist for several reasons:

- A relatively high level of domestic tax rate is applied to a gross amount of royalties;
- The tax rate is not usually reduced much under tax treaties;
- Even in cases where tax treaty benefits for royalties are applied, the process of obtaining such treaty benefits is based on special request submitted to tax authorities by the taxpayer;
- A higher tax treaty rate for royalties is primarily applied in tax treaties with developed states, while lower rates are applied under treaties with the developing world (Worldwide Tax Summaries Online 2020).

Therefore, Egypt's approach towards taxation of royalties at source creates a fiscal barrier for attracting foreign IP, intangibles and know-how into the local economy, which is especially critical for sustainable digital transformation. Tax is withheld from the gross amount, so R&D costs incurred by the foreign taxpayer are not taken into consideration, therefore licensors' profits can be small in relation to the size of royalties paid (UN 2018). In such situations, the burden of tax is likely included in the amount of royalties and is economically passed to the local licensee. More open tax treaty policy in relation to royalties can potentially contribute to digital development in Egypt.

General conclusive note and three tax policy proposals on the way forwards for Africa

Conclusive note

Answering the question that was incorporated in the title of this research article, Africa needs a customised approach for reforming its tax legislation in line with the emerging digital reality. A key reason for this is the strikingly different level of economic development and digital readiness between the few leaders of the continent and the other states. This suggestion is supported by the analysis of the key economic and digital transformation indicators across the set of African economies and the discussion of trends in tax reforms at the domestic and international levels.

At the same time, another important result of the discussion of tax cooperation and tax competition trends in this article is the observation that even being very different from one another, African countries have no other way to defend their sovereign economic interests in global economic regulation levels besides deep cooperation with one another. Otherwise, larger and more powerful economies defining the international tax policy agenda at the OECD level can ignore the priorities of African countries when designing international tax reform in relation to the digital economy.

On this basis, we propose several ideas for further digitally related tax reforms in the delineated groups of African countries, including leaders, emerging leaders and other states. We also suggest two scenarios for tax cooperation between the African states and other states and insist on the consistency between the two discussed research results. The overall direction of the desirable international tax policy in relation to digital business in Africa can be summarised in a simple formula: targeted approach for the leaders, cooperation for everyone.

The leader takes all, even in Africa: digital reform proposals for South Africa

As was discussed in the fifth section, one of the pressing issues for South Africa is ensuring taxation at the residence state of its digitalised businesses. This issue is also problematic in case of dual residency conflict under tax treaties with developed foreign states. As the OECD notices in the digital environment application of POEM, the concept can lead to controversial results and not eliminate legal uncertainty because some evidence of nexus with both states can exist (OECD 2001). The OECD recommends having a mutual agreement procedure between the competent authorities in this case to determine the tax residency of the company (OECD 2008).

However, the authors' recommendation for South Africa in this regard is to introduce economic criteria for determining the POEM of a company, especially in the digital context. Such economic analysis can include accounting for such factors as the level of the economic ties, the amount a company's economic resources are used in different countries, personal nexus of its key management team and the use of legal, financial, physical and social infrastructure in different countries. For digital businesses, it is reasonable to consider the level of the company's reliance on the digital users residing in the country as one of the crucial factors. Such analysis can be used for determining the corporate residence of companies who are part of the largest MNEs based on the information from country-by-country reports about international distribution of key economic indicators of MNEs' performance.

Following the leader: recommendations for the emerging African digital leaders (Group 2 states)

One of the important future reforms for Egypt and other North African states from Group 2 (Tunisia, Morocco) can be introducing a more open policy in relation to royalties. Such an approach can be developed by considering some part of R&D costs incurred by the licensor in the local economy. This can be done through the 'interim' withholding tax mechanism, where a non-resident can subsequently credit R&D costs against royalty income received, if such costs are incurred in the source country (Trepelkov, Tonino, and Halka 2015).

Such a mechanism can contribute to achieving two tax policy goals: incentivising outsourcing R&D functions by non-residents to local companies and ensuring taxation of royalty income closer to a net basis. The proposed reform can be accompanied by detailed administrative and compliance practices, such as, for example, special forms of reporting to tax authorities about such R&D costs incurred by non-residents in the local economy. This is based on the idea of disclosure of certain potentially aggressive transactions to tax authorities, as proposed by the OECD in BEPS Action 12 (2015). Therefore, African source countries can obtain a flexible instrument of attracting foreign IP and other intangible assets that are necessary for the advanced digital transformation of their economies.

In unity is our strength: recommendations for cooperation among the least developed and more developed African countries

As follows from the analysis of arguments around these unilateral or multilateral reforms, each digital tax reform has important pros and cons. However, the crucial interest for African states is to get as much revenue as possible with minimum administrative effort and minimum barriers for the digital transformation. We suggest two basic tax reform scenarios in this regard.

Coordination of tax policy between the African countries to increase the bargaining power of Africa at global tax policy discussion at the OECD on Pillar 1

A coordinated position can be targeted at increasing the role of market states in taxing digitalised businesses at the source. Such a position can also be in line with the interests of the other developing and emerging large economies, such as Brazil, Russia, India, China, South Africa (BRICS) economies. In this scenario, no unilateral measure such as DST is necessary. The key problem of such a policy is that even together, the economic share of African states is still too little for lobbying and bargaining at the global governance level or to compete with developed countries. Therefore, such coordination efforts can only work in case of cooperation with the other emerging/developing economies and can take a long time to achieve the necessary progress.

Coordination of tax policy between the African countries to introduce DST in a harmonised tax policy reform

This unilateral interim measure can address the current urgent revenue financing needs in transition time when the OECD Pillar 1 proposal is still not introduced globally. This tax policy move seems practically feasible because some African states already have experience in introducing domestic DST and ATAF have worked on model DST rules, which can be a basis for such inter-African tax (ATAF 2020b). A key advantage of such a tax policy is the creation of a level playing field in the digital arena inside the overall African market. Such a proposal is also in line with the current trends in African trade policy, such as the African Continental Free Trade Agreement, which, according to study by World Bank, has enormous economic potential for the region in reducing the poverty and increasing the wealth of African nations (World Bank 2020).

While engaging in tax policy bargaining with developed states can be an irrational idea for developing African countries because of the inherent economic inequality, introducing coordinated DST throughout Africa can nevertheless be a good tax policy option, especially as an interim measure reflecting a compromise position between African states and the developed world. There are several arguments for this idea. First, DST creates minimal barriers and distortions for intra-African and third-country trade in digital services because of its low rates and simple mechanics; second, such a policy can work as a preventive measure against international tax competition among African countries for the location of headquarters of digitalised businesses. Nevertheless, there are still several administrative and technical problems of 'coordinated DST' policy because administering and enforcing DST payment by non-resident digitalised businesses still need advanced levels of technical capacity, as it is based not on a withholding mechanism but on tax return submission by non-residents. Moreover, it is still unclear how DST fits into the system of the existing international tax and trade agreements, as it is a relatively new and controversial legal development; therefore, legal uncertainty can potentially arise for taxpayers.

Note

1. Today, the OECD acts as a global leader in coordinating international tax policy development. To a lesser extent, this statement applies to the United Nations (UN) (including the United Nations Conference on Trade and Development (UNCTAD)).

Disclosure statement

No potential conflict of interest was reported by the author(s).

Funding

This research is performed under the state assignment (funding) of RANEPA.

References

Ainsworth, R. T., and A. Shact. 2014. "Transfer pricing: UN practical manual–China." Public Law Research Paper (No. 14-1), Boston University. Accessed October 5, 2021. http://dx.doi.org/10.2139/ssrn.2375785.

Asen, Elke. 2021. "What European OECD countries are doing about Digital Services Taxes?" *TaxFoundation*, June 20. Accessed October 5, 2021. https://taxfoundation.org/digital-tax-europe-2020/.

Aslam, Aqib, and Alpa Shah. 2020. "Tec(h)tonic shifts: Taxing the "digital economy"." IMF Working Papers (№ 20/76). Accessed October 5, 2021. https://www.elibrary.imf.org/view/journals/001/2020/076/article-A001-en.xml.

ATAF (African Tax Administration Forum). 2009. "ATAF model tax agreement for the avoidance of double taxation and the prevention of fiscal evasion in respect of taxes on income." Accessed October 5, 2021. https://events.ataftax.org/events/index.php?page=documents&func=view&document_id=7.

ATAF (African Tax Administration Forum). 2019. "The tax challenges arising in Africa from the digitalisation of the economy." Accessed October 5, 2021. https://irp-cdn.multiscreensite.com/a521d626/files/uploaded/Tech%20Note%2017012019.pdf.

ATAF (African Tax Administration Forum). 2020a. "Domestic resource mobilization (Digital services taxation in Africa)." Accessed October 5, 2021. https://events.ataftax.org/index.php?page=documents&func=view&document_id=61.

ATAF (African Tax Administration Forum). 2020b. "Suggested approach to drafting digital services tax legislation." Accessed October 5, 2021. https://events.ataftax.org/index.php?page=documents&func=view&document_id=79.

Brauner, Y. 2016. "Treaties in the Aftermath of BEPS." *Brooklyn Journal of International Law* 41 (3): 973–1041.

Broekhuijsen, D., and H. Vording. 2016. "The Multilateral tax Instrument: How to Avoid a Stalemate on Distributional Issues?" *British Tax Review* 1: 39–61.

Businesstech. 2020. "New proposal for South Africa to tax digital services like Netflix and Spotify." June 19. Accessed October 5, 2021. https://businesstech.co.za/news/finance/406151/new-proposal-for-south-africa-to-tax-digital-services-like-netflix-and-spotify/.

Coleman, Colin. 2020. "This region will be worth $5.6 trillion within 5 years – but only if it accelerates its policy reforms." *World Economic Forum*, February 11. Accessed October 5, 2021. https://www.weforum.org/agenda/2020/02/africa-global-growth-economics-worldwide-gdp/.

Cruz Cano, Mattias. 2020. "COVID-19 will reshape African tax landscape." *International Tax Review*, May 18. Accessed October 5, 2021. https://www.internationaltaxreview.com/article/b1lp2jlt7p0f7 m/covid-19-will-reshape-african-tax-landscape.

Dagan, T. 2017. "The Future of Corporate Residency". Research Paper (№ 18-14), Bar-Ilan University. Accessed October 5, 2021. https://law.huji.ac.il/sites/default/files/law/files/the_future_of_corporate_residence.pdf.

Deloitte tax at hand. 2020. "Digital services tax in Africa: The journey so far." August 13. Accessed October 5, 2021https://www.taxathand.com/article/15137/Egypt/2020/Digital-services-tax-in-Africa-The-journey-so-far.

El-Kamel, Moamen. 2019. "Digital taxation push raises eyebrows in Egypt." *Al-Monitor*, September 6. Accessed October 5, 2021. https://www.al-monitor.com/pulse/originals/2019/08/egypt-facebook-e-commerce-draft-law-companies-advertisers.html.

Fitch Solutions. 2018. "Egypt information technology report." https://nations-emergentes.org/wp-content/uploads/2019/02/egypt-information-technoly.pdf.

Global 500. 2020. "Fortune." Accessed October 5, 2021. https://fortune.com/global500/.

Gross domestic product. 2019. "E-Handbook of statistics." UNCTAD. Accessed October 5, 2021https://stats.unctad.org/Handbook/EconomicTrends/Gdp.html.

Hoke, William. 2019. "Analysts evaluate Israel tax authority's plans for a digital tax." *Pearl Cohen*, May 19. Accessed October 5, 2021. https://www.pearlcohen.com/analysts-evaluate-israel-tax-authoritys-plans-for-a-digital/.

Hufbauer, Gary Clyde. 2020. "Making global corporate giants pay their fair share of taxes." *Peterson Institute for International Economics*, March 12. Accessed October 5, 2021https://www.piie.com/blogs/realtime-economic-issues-watch/making-global-corporate-giants-pay-their-fair-share-taxes.

International Tax Review. 2019. "Does India's proposals on attribution of profits to PEs solve the issue?" May 20. Accessed October 5, 2021. https://www.internationaltaxreview.com/article/b1fq9g90kbsyzv/does-indias-proposals-on-attribution-of-profits-to-pes-solve-the-issue.

Leigh, Thomas. 2020. "Britain and France suggest phased approach to global digital tax talks." *Reuters*, June 26. Accessed October 5, 2021. https://uk.reuters.com/article/us-usa-trade-digital/britain-and-france-suggest-phased-approach-to-global-digital-tax-talks-idUKKBN23X132.

Martin, Julie. 2019. Is the US about to blow up the OECD's compromise "Pillar One" plan for taxing multinational group profit?" MNE Tax, December 5. Accessed October 5, 2021. https://mnetax.com/is-the-us-about-to-blow-up-the-oecds-compromise-pillar-one-plan-for-taxing-multinationals-profit-36960.

Monkam, N., G. Ibrahim, W. Davis, and C. von Haldenwang. 2019. "Tax challenges of digitalization in Africa." Accessed October 5, 2021. https://www.g20-insights.org/wp-content/uploads/2019/05/t20-japan-tf5-6-tax-challenges-digitalization-africa-1.pdf.

Moore, M. 2020. *What Is Wrong with African Tax Administration? ICTD Working Paper 111*. Brighton: Institute of Development Studies.

Obayemi, O. 2021. "Country Note: Taxing The Income Of Digital Non-Resident Companies Under The 'Significant Economic Presence' (Sep) Rules In Nigeria." *Intertax* 49 (5): 449–465.

OECD (Organisation for Economic Cooperation and Development). 2001. "The impact of the communications revolution on the application of "place of effective management" as a tie breaker rule." Accessed October 5, 2021. http://www.oecd.org/ctp/treaties/1923328.pdf.

OECD (Organisation for Economic Cooperation and Development). 2008. "Draft contents of the 2008 update to the Model Tax Convention." Accessed October 5, 2021. http://www.oecd.org/ctp/treaties/40489100.pdf.

OECD (Organisation for Economic Cooperation and Development). 2015. *Mandatory Disclosure Rules, Action 12 - 2015 Final Report*. Paris: OECD Publishing.

OECD (Organisation for Economic Cooperation and Development). 2017a. *Model Tax Convention on Income and On Capital: Condensed Version 2017*. Paris: OECD Publishing.

OECD (Organisation for Economic Cooperation and Development). 2017b. *OECD Transfer Pricing Guidelines for Multinational Enterprises and Tax Administrations 2017*. Paris: OECD Publishing.

OECD (Organisation for Economic Cooperation and Development). 2019. "Secretariat proposal for a "unified approach" under Pillar One." Accessed October 5, 2021. https://www.oecd.org/tax/beps/public-consultation-document-secretariat-proposal-unified-approach-pillar-one.pdf.

OECD (Organisation for Economic Cooperation and Development). 2020. *OECD Investment Policy Reviews: Egypt 2020*. Paris: OECD Publishing.

OECD (Organisation for Economic Cooperation and Development). 2021. "Addressing the tax challenges arising from the digitalisation of the economy." Accessed October 5, 2021. https://www.oecd.org/tax/beps/brochure-addressing-the-tax-challenges-arising-from-the-digitalisation-of-the-economy-july-2021.pdf.

Overall ranking and data tables. "Paying Taxes 2020, PwC." https://www.pwc.com/gx/en/services/tax/publications/paying-taxes-2020/overall-ranking-and-data-tables.html (accessed October 5, 2021).

Sarfo, Nana Amo. 2020. "Digital taxation in Africa: Safety in numbers?" Forbes, September 22. https://www.forbes.com/sites/taxnotes/2020/09/22/digital-taxation-in-africa-safety-in-numbers/?sh=3d2f89ab31a7 (accessed October 5, 2021).

South African Revenue Service. 2015. Interpretation Note: No. 6 (Issue 2).

Trepelkov, A., H. Tonino, and D. Halka. 2015. *United Nations Handbook on Selected Issues in Protecting the Tax Base of Developing Countries*. New York: United Nations.

UNCTAD (United Nations Conference on Trade and Development). 2019. B2C e-commerce index. Accessed October 5, 2021. https://unctad.org/system/files/official-document/tn_unctad_ict4d14_en.pdf.

UNCTAD (United Nations Conference on Trade and Development). 2020. *World Investment Report: International Production Beyond the Pandemic*. Geneva: United Nations.

UN (United Nations). 2014a. *BEPS questionnaire Ghana*. Accessed October 5, 2021. https://www.un.org/esa/ffd/wp-content/uploads/2014/10/ta-BEPS-CommentsGhana.pdf.

UN (United Nations). 2014b. *BEPS comments Lesotho*. Accessed October 5, 2021. https://www.un.org/esa/ffd/wp-content/uploads/2014/12/ta-BEPS-CommentsLesotho.pdf.

UN (United Nations). 2014c. *Responses to questionnaire for developing countries from the UN Subcommittee on Base Erosion and Profit Shifting*. Accessed October 5, 2021. https://www.un.org/esa/ffd/wp-content/uploads/2014/10/10STM_CRP12_BEPS1.pdf.

UN (United Nations). 2018. *United Nations Model Double Taxation Convention Between Developed and Developing Countries: 2017 Update*. New York: United Nations.

UN (United Nations). 2019. *Tax Issues related to the Digitalization of the Economy: Report*. Accessed October 5, 2021. https://www.un.org/esa/ffd/wp-content/uploads/2019/04/18STM_CRP12-Work-on-taxation-issues-digitalization.pdf.

Van Zyl, Jana. 2020. "Taxation in South Africa: Does it even matter where my company is registered?" *Go Legal*, March 5. Accessed October 5, 2021. https://www.golegal.co.za/place-effective-management-offshore/.

World Bank. 2018. *Mashreq 2.0: Digital Transformation for Inclusive Growth and Jobs*. Washington, DC: World Bank.

World Bank. 2020. *The African Continental Free Trade Area: Economic and Distributional Effects*. Washington, DC: World Bank.

World Bank Open Data. 2020a. "Charges for the Use of Intellectual Property, Receipts (BoP, current US$)." Accessed October 5, 2021. https://data.worldbank.org/indicator/BX.GSR.ROYL.CD.

World Bank Open Data. 2020b. "Charges for the Use of Intellectual Property, Payments (BoP, current US$)." Accessed October 5, 2021. https://data.worldbank.org/indicator/BM.GSR.ROYL.CD.

World Bank Open Data. 2020c. "Individuals Using the Internet (% of population)." Accessed October 5, 2021. https://data.worldbank.org/indicator/IT.NET.USER.ZS.

Worldwide Tax Summaries Online. 2020. PricewaterhouseCoopers. Accessed October 5, 2021. https://taxsummaries.pwc.com/.

Intellectual property rights, agricultural biotechnology and food sufficiency: strengthening the Nigerian intellectual property legal framework for food self-sufficiency in the aftermath of Global Pandemic

Helen Chuma-Okoro and Ifeoma Ann Oluwasemilore

ABSTRACT
This article focuses on the imperatives of self-sufficiency in food production in Nigeria from the experience of the COVID 19 pandemic, and examines the role of intellectual property rights (IPRS) in boosting productive capacity. While the different types of IPR protection standards remain relevant to the overall goal of food self-sufficiency in respect of the different activities and outputs along the food value chain, the main emphasis of the article is on patent and plant varieties protection (PVP) in connection with agricultural biotechnology. The article is library-based and explains the meaning and import of food self-sufficiency, the factors responsible for the weak capacity for food self-sufficiency in Nigeria in particular, and other African countries vis-à-vis potentially enabling factors. It also examines the strength and weaknesses of the current IP laws in Nigeria, and how Nigeria could repurpose or improve her laws to achieve the objective of food self-sufficiency. The article found that IPRs are relevant in boosting greater efficiency and productivity of Nigerian agriculture to strengthen food self-sufficiency, but the current IPR framework are not designed to circumvent the perils and leverage the benefits of IPRs that would help unlock the potential of the sector for food self-sufficiency.

1. Background

If there is one vital message to the world in the year 2020, it is the importance of being self-sufficient in meeting their essential needs. The COVID-19 pandemic has had severe impacts on almost all facets of the society, causing major disruptions in activities across the world. One of such disruptions concerned the movement of persons and goods as countries closed their borders and imposed lockdowns within to curtail the spread of the virus while awaiting an effective vaccine (ASM 2020). The resultant shortages in basic items, including food in African countries (Laborde et al. 2020), underscores the importance of self-sufficiency in productive capacity, especially for African countries with generally high dependency on imported food. It is estimated that African countries spend a total of 35 billion United States (US) Dollars a year on importing food which they should be producing (Agency Report 2017), and access to food is highly dependent on cross-border markets (Spore 2017).

While the COVID-19 related worries concerning availability of food due to the disruption of food production supply chains could be addressed through strategic measures (ASM 2020; Laborde et al. 2020), such as, exemptions for essential activities, including the transportation of food stuffs, there is little a country could do about barriers to foreign food supplies other than reliance on self-production, of which agricultural inputs, including seeds, are the starting point. Breakthroughs in agricultural biotechnology (agritech) have seen great improvements in food availability and affordability for the world's population. Agritech is the 'core of agricultural innovation on which food supply and agricultural products depend' (Adebola 2018). But the importance of agritech and its impact on food production cannot be contemplated without reference to the role of intellectual property rights (IPRs).

IPRs operate as legal and policy standards for rewarding creativity and innovative efforts (Merges, Menell, and Lemley 2000, 319–320). They are a prerequisite for commercialising and protecting inventions against unauthorised exploitation by third parties. Once applicable, the invention can only be exploited with the owner's authorisation usually obtained at a fee. Thus, IPRs provide incentives for investing in research, development and diffusion of inventions (WIPO n.d.). This critical role of IPRs also extends to agritech, and the manner in which IPRs operate could have significant implications for food self-sufficiency and food security (Haugen, Muller, and Narasimhan 2010). Indeed, the extension of IPRs to agritech is of increasing import in the global discourse on food not only in terms of encouraging innovations in improved seeds, but also in relation to access to such innovations (Spore 2017). As Gollin noted, 'intellectual property creates winners and losers and on balance it helps in some situations, hurts in others' (Spore 2017). The continuous expansion of the landscape of IPRs to accommodate new inventions in agriculture has enormous impact on food availability and affordability, particularly patents and plant variety protection (PVP) (Gollin 2008). Designing the IPR framework towards boosting agricultural productivity as a foundational strategy to strengthen food self-sufficiency in Africa is therefore essential.

With focus on Nigeria, this article elucidates the importance of self-sufficiency and the role of IPRs in achieving food self-sufficiency. It underscores the imperative with reference to experiences from the COVID-19 pandemic. It recognises that, among other things, achieving food self-sufficiency depends on technological capacity, particularly agritech which is galvanised by IPRs. Therefore, understanding the major implications of the interface between IPRs and agritech is relevant in construing the right IPR framework for achieving food self-sufficiency. It also examines the concerns and implications for African countries over the extension of protection to agritech in the global IPR framework, and also the existing Nigerian IPR framework for achieving food self-sufficiency. It proffers solutions for improvement of the Nigerian framework.

2. Food self-sufficiency and the covid-19 pandemic

2.1. Food self-sufficiency

Food is a basic necessity for life. But food is not just important as what we eat in order to survive. Different foods fulfil a wide variety of roles in our lives beyond sustenance, including physiological, social and cultural values (Tansey 2008, 7). There is a marked difference between food self-sufficiency and food security as a fundamental human right which should be guaranteed to every human, with foundations in the Universal Declaration of Human Rights (UDHR). The UDHR provides that '[e]veryone has the right to a standard of living adequate for the health and well-being of himself and his family including food ... ' (Preamble para. 5, Article 25). In the words of former United Nations (UN) Secretary General, Kofi Annan, the right to food is 'the most basic human rights of all,' (UN Doc. UNIS/SG/2685) and includes both concepts of adequate food and the right to be free from hunger (Niada 2006). The UN Special Rapporteur on the Right to Food, Hilal Elver, explains the right to food more broadly noting that

> the right to food is the right to have regular, permanent and unrestricted access either directly or by means of financial purchases to quantitatively and qualitatively adequate and sufficient food corresponding to the cultural traditions of the people to which the consumer belongs, and which ensure a physical and mental, individual and collective, fulfilling and dignified life free of fear. (UN Human Rights Office of the High Commission)

There is a specific understanding to what being food secured entails which underscores the fact that food security is achieved only when 'all people,' including the poor, have access to safe, sufficient and nutritious food at all times and are free from hunger (Rome Declaration 1996), regardless of their circumstances, including prisoners of war, (Article 26), Convention III of the Geneva Conventions (1949); civilians in conflict situations, (Article 29), Geneva Convention (IV); and children, (Article 24), Convention on the Rights of the Child. The global community has reaffirmed through the UN Millennium Declaration their commitment to eradicate poverty and to reduce the number of persons suffering from hunger. (UN Millennium Declaration, G.A. Res. 55/2, 3, U.N. GAOR, Para.19). This commitment was given further impetus as a key arm of the Millennium Development Goals (MDGs) now revitalised in the 2030 Agenda for Sustainable Development Goals (SDGs). SDG 2 focuses explicitly on seeking to 'end hunger, achieve food security and improved nutrition and promote sustainable agriculture.' (SDG Compass)

On the whole, food security requires that food must be available in sufficient quantity as needed, affordable *and* safe for human consumption, whether sourced locally or imported. Taken from this broad perspective, food security requires tackling factors that undermine availability, affordability and adequacy, (Interim Report of the Special Rapporteur on the Right to Food) and promote greater productivity along the food value chain. Food insecurity occurs 'when people lack secure access to sufficient amounts of safe and nutritious food' (FAO, IFAD and WFP 2013, 50).

Unlike food security, the concept of food self-sufficiency lays emphasis on the source of food. According to the UN Food and Agriculture Organisation (FAO), self-sufficiency 'typically refers to countries that seek to produce all or most of their own food for domestic consumption' (FAO 2015–2016). However, no matter their level of self-sufficiency, all countries typically import some foods. Thus the more realistic conception of food self-sufficiency is a continuum between complete self-reliance and full liberalisation with reference to a country's domestic food market (Clapp 2017; FAO 2015–16, 2–7). As such, FAO defines food self-sufficiency as 'the extent to which a country can satisfy its food needs from its own domestic production' along a continuum of what it terms the 'self-sufficiency ratio (SSR),' measured in the ratio of a country's food production to its food consumption (FAO 1999, para: 4.2.1). Following this formula, it concluded that food self-sufficiency only requires a country to produce enough or more food than it consumes even if imported food also forms part of the aggregate food consumption (FAO, 2–3; Clapp 2017, 89).

The marked difference between the two concepts is the fact that while food security can be achieved through local production, international market sources or aid programmes, food self-sufficiency relies mainly on own production (Minot and Pelijor 2010, 1; FAO 1999). Thus a country could be food secured without being food self-sufficient. But any country with an excess of food demand over its supply is not self-sufficient, and therefore ultimately food insecure (Osabohien, Osabuohien, and Urhie 2017). Proponents of self-sufficiency consider it important to curb the risk of depending on imports which is prone to market instability in relation to prices and supplies, as well as other political and economic driven external pressures. For them, achieving food security through improved local farming methods presents a much safer approach (FAO 2015–16, 7). Conversely, critics of self-sufficiency consider self-reliance costly due to inefficiencies in the use of resources by a country that may arise from lack of greater specialisation in the production of food items with high comparative advantage (Clapp 2017).

Regardless of this conflicting positions, it is generally accepted that national self-sufficiency is an important safeguard for a country's dietary needs at all times irrespective of external circumstances and contingencies such as war and market instability. As O'Hagan (1976, 359) noted, countries see self-sufficiency as a politically pragmatic policy safeguard against negative repercussions and vulnerability in depending on other countries for their food supply in a world driven by political interests. The COVID-19 pandemic exemplifies other contingencies that could affect a country's food supplies and threaten food security. Whether in the context of food security or food self-sufficiency, the ultimate concern is for people to have sufficient food to meet their daily nutritional needs at all times.

2.2. Food self-sufficiency and COVID-19 in Nigeria

Like other countries, Nigeria's primary response to the COVID-19 pandemic was to impose various levels of lockdown across the country for an initial period of over six months, including a ban on international and domestic air travels (Ibrahim, Ajide, and Julius 2020; Adebowale 2020). This affected activities in all sectors including the food sector with short and long term impacts on food production, supplies and distribution (Penrhys-Evan 2020; Schlein 2020; Aday and Aday 2020). Underscoring an important lesson from the phenomenon, President Mohammadu Buhari noted thus: '[t]he Coronavirus pandemic has illustrated more than any event in recent history how countries must strive harder to protect food systems. It has also exposed the limits of dependency on other countries' (State House 2020).

Even before the pandemic, Nigeria, like other African countries, had been grappling with inadequate food supplies to serve local needs, despite its past records of high food productivity (Punch 2020). Many Nigerians today lack access to adequate, affordable and nutritious food (Obonyilo 2008). As at 2017, one in four Nigerians was severely affected by inadequate food access (Bakare 2018). Reports show that the number of food insecure people in Nigeria has doubled from 23 million to 50 million between 2018 and 2021 (NESG 2021), indicating an alarming rate of declining access to food.

Generally, African countries experience low production capacities in their basic needs including food (FAO 2017; Baer-Nawrocka and Sadowski 2019). Rocca and Schultes (2020, 1) note that Africa remains heavily dependent on food imports despite the high percentage of people employed in the agricultural sector. Of the 10 worst food crisis recorded globally in 2019, five occurred in Africa specifically in the Democratic Republic of Congo, Ethiopia, South Sudan, Sudan and Northern Nigeria. Sub-Saharan Africa was marked as the world's most food insecure region even before COVID-19 (Rocca and Schultes 2020). For these countries and regions therefore, the COVID-19 pandemic aggravates an already critical food situation (World Bank 2021). Experts have warned that the world should brace up for more of pandemics due to long-term damages to the environment (Vaughan 2019).

There are other dynamics outside the COVID-19 induced lockdowns that create further concerns for Nigeria in relying more on importation for local food supplies. This means that even with the lifting of lockdowns and cross-border travel restrictions, sourcing food from abroad would remain a challenge for both the government and its citizens. Nigeria has been import dependent since the 1980s, with an estimated expenditure of $3 billion annually on food importation. According to the World Bank (GAIN 2020, 6), even before the pandemic, foreign reserves had been dropping with an accumulated loss of $11 billion between June 2019 and May 2020. In 2019, $1.09 billion, $406 billion and $199 billion were spent on wheat, sugar and palm oil respectively despite the fact that these products are also produced locally (Punch 2020). However, dwindling resources caused by the pandemic has reduced purchasing power for the average Nigerian, while the devaluation of the Nigerian currency makes government subsidy for food importation unsustainable (GAIN 2020, 6).

Just recently, the Nigerian government directed the Agriculture Promotion Policy, APP (2016–2020), towards growing the agricultural sector with focus on improving local production based on an import ban policy (FMARD 2016, 5). However, despite the benefits to local farmers, banning the importation of staples like rice without local production in sufficient quantities to meet local demand is counter-productive to the achievement of food sufficiency (Bakare 2018). As part of measures to help achieve food security in the country, President Buhari has emphasised the imperative of focusing on improving yield per hectare as much as increasing hectares under cultivation (State House 2020).

The factors affecting local food production are myriad, with conflicts between farmers and Herdsmen among them (Osabohien, Osabuohien, and Urhie 2017, 5). Therefore, the food situation in Nigeria is projected to increase given the deteriorating conflict situation in the country, while a rapidly growing population projected to hit 400 million by 2050 portends drastic increase in demand for food (NESG 2021). These dynamics make measures to achieve greater efficiency in farm productivity highly imperative. There are reasons to believe Nigeria has the potential to achieve food-sufficiency, including: vast arable land mass; abundant water resources; favourable climatic conditions; and rich biodiversity (Kuhlmann et al. 2018; FMARD 2016). But without the right technological knowhow, these resources cannot be fully harnessed to achieve increased productivity. Oftentimes, a lot of value is lost both in quantity and quality of food before it gets to the market. For instance, 40–50% of tomato produced in Nigeria is lost due to the poor handling, processing and preservation practices, which makes innovations focused on reducing post-harvest losses essential (Sahel 2017). Lack of capacity to add value to agricultural yields diminishes the choices of food items available to the people, and the quantity of food supply (Barakat Mahmoud 2018).

2.3. IPRs for food self-sufficiency

2.3.1. General overview/background

IPRs refer to the group of legal regimes -notably patents, trademarks, copyright, and utility designs, which reward various creative and innovation activities by protecting the outputs of such activities, in order to encourage more production (WIPO 2004, n.d.). These different forms of IPRs provide creators and inventors with legal protection from the misappropriation of their intellectual output by granting the owners monopoly rights of control over use. The different types of IPRs may be linked to the different activities that may occur along the food value chain, and exploited accordingly. For instance, copyright, which protects literary works and other creative works of expression would protect the various publications, promotional and info materials developed by businesses for their use, including manuals, brochures, and software (WIPO 2004, 40–67). The same applies to utility designs, which protects the aesthetic qualities of functional products, such as, farming tools and product packages (WIPO 2004, 112–118). Additionally, agribusinesses rely on good marketing and competitiveness for which trademarks are useful. Trademark refers to names, symbols, colours, or shapes used to distinguish products in the market. The sole purpose of trademarks is to protect investments in building product goodwill based on quality (WIPO 2004, 67–105).

However, where technological innovation is concern, patents are key, in addition to PVP rights in the case of agritech. Patents are temporary legal privileges granted to an inventor to prevent the public from producing, using or selling the invention without the inventor's consent (WIPO 2004). Innovations in seed technology involve investments in technological knowhow. Studies have shown that technology is a critical enabler needed to transform Africa's agricultural sector to provide abundant, quality and affordable food to its growing population (Sahel Quarterly 2021, 4–31). Unfortunately, use of technology in agriculture is still at its infancy in Africa where farming is largely subsistence and methods are largely elementary.

2.3.2. IPRs and food self-sufficiency in Nigeria

The relevance of IPRs in achieving food self-sufficiency in Nigeria is mainly derived from the role of IPRs as the dominant framework for rewarding and encouraging innovation, including agritech. The American Seed Trade Industry notes that '[s]trong intellectual property protection allows developers of new plant varieties and improved seeds to be rewarded for their efforts' and that 'this promotes research and development, which ultimately enhances crop production and conservation of genetic resources' (Kuyek 2002, 2).

For developing countries like Nigeria with typically low innovation capacity, effective IP systems are necessary to attract foreign direct investment (FDI), encourage technology transfer, support a research and development (R&D) and maintain capacity for local food production and innovation in all spheres of the agricultural ecosystem. Therefore, an effective and trusted IPR system can help achieve food self-sufficiency by helping to boost agricultural productivity.

But IPRs also 'impose hidden costs on the same scale' and so must be carefully considered (Gollin 2008, 1). For instance, as Gollin (2008, 15) explained, the 'IP system also determines when and how an innovation becomes available for others to use by defining boundaries around what is accessible and what is not'. On this basis, IPRs could adversely affect a country like Nigeria and her self-sufficiency capability by restricting access to much needed protected innovation of foreign origin. For the smallholder farmer, affordability becomes the major determinant for access even for Nigerian made technologies. Therefore, IPRs could portend both promises and perils on Nigeria's food self-sufficiency and food security objectives. Unless properly calibrated, IPRs could hinder the goals of ensuring food self-sufficiency in Africa, including Nigeria.

The farming system in Nigeria is both formal and informal with a larger proportion of informal dominated by smallholder famers while the former sector comprised of corporate plant breeders. For the players operating within these two different ecosystems, IPRs may not have the same implications. Protecting and leveraging these layers of innovations therefore arises as a major challenge in designing an effective IP system. Like most African countries,

The smallholder farmers practice mainly subsistence farming following processes drawn from old traditions. Over 90% of their seeds are sourced from within their communities (Kuyek 2002, 2). African smallholder farmers, described as 'Africa's silent innovators' (Kuyek 2002, 4), have managed to sustain and improve on their traditional agricultural knowledge through ingenuity in seed selection or plant breeding involving a meticulous process of selection. On this basis, it has been observed that 'small farmers constitute Africa's most important and most capable innovators' (Kuyek 2002, 4). Yet the ingenuity of the African small farmer as a plant breeder is not adequately rewarded under Western modelled IP framework, partly because their kind of plant breeding innovation does not fit the criteria for protection under conventional IP laws.

This contrasts sharply with the case of the corporate plant breeder in the formal private contributing to seed breeding in the African agricultural setting. For these categories of innovators, IPRs are of high priority to reward the heavy investment in R&D. Lack of effective guarantees of IPR protection could discourage investments in the agricultural sector by these entities. Generally, the multilateral companies do not share the same interests or challenges with the smallholder farmers. For instance, multilateral plant breeding pay more attention to developing plant varieties of crops with high commercial returns, such as wheat, rice and maize, leaving out other lesser known crops cultivated by small farmers enriching the food basket of Africa which could also benefit from innovative processes to develop better yielding seeds (Oguamanam 2015).

2.3.3. Patents

Given the incentivizing rationale behind their existence, patents are of great importance to the agricultural biotechnological industry and indeed the food value chain. Generally, a patentable invention must satisfy specific conditions which simply mean that it must be novel, useful and non-obvious to an ordinary person (WIPO 2004, 17).

There is great discrepancy in the scope of the subject matter that can be patented across jurisdictions. Traditionally, patents were not extended to agricultural life forms following an underlying perception that the link between basic food needs and agriculture made commercialisation undesirable. However, the advent of biotechnology has seen the extension of patents to micro-organisms (including new plant varieties), and all life forms in countries like the US, mainly as necessary to reward and encourage the huge investments involved in R&D (Perkins, 99). Nevertheless, the extension of patents to plant variety remains unpopular and has been rejected as a strategy for developing their seed industry by most countries, including all European countries (Dutfield 2008, 39).

2.3.4. Plant variety protection right (PVP)

PVP for agricultural life forms is also relatively new. PVP is traceable to mid-1900 when the US and some countries in Europe started recognising limited protection for new plant variety in favour of their breeders (Thippeswamy 2017).

As an IP, plant variety has a specific meaning which distinguishes it from other kinds of seeds. However, the true definition differs in scope globally. As IP, plant varieties centres around varieties developed through biotechnology. Broadly, protection serves as reward to breeder for their effort or investments in developing the variety (Bakare 2018). While the rationale for such a reward is not normally contested, agreeing on a universal template remains elusive, mainly because of interests between smallholders and cooperate breeders. These divergences gives rise to two different, largely competing kinds of rights which should be balanced: namely, the plant breeders' (monopoly) right (PBR) and the farmer's privilege. The PBR is a monopoly right because it protects certain uses which cannot be made of their variety without their authorisation, subject to exceptions (Dutfield 2008).

However, like patenting of germplasm, developing countries tend to resist PBR as not relevant to their kind of informal and open collaborative agricultural systems (Muredzi and Sackey 1995, 24, 99) On the whole, three main approaches exist for protecting new plant varieties: patent, PVP rights and *sui generis* rights.

2.3.5. Farmer's rights

Farmers' right as a part of the IPR framework arises from their longstanding role in domesticating wild plants and making them suitable for cultivation through plant breeding (Anderson 2005). The conception of farmer's right which should be protected stems from the need to not only reward their ingenuity and longstanding effort in developing indigenous varieties, but to also encourage them to continue their activities in situ for the sustenance of plant genetic diversity (Anderson 2005, 129; Muredzi and Sackey 1995, 99). However, this entitlement is mostly given as an exception to the PBR in what is known as the farmers' privilege, mainly allowing them to save and replant seeds.

3. The international IP framework for food self-sufficiency from the African perspective

The international framework for food self-sufficiency is fundamentally a reflection of the conflicts and dichotomies arising between African countries and developed countries in the extension of IPRs to agricultural biotechnology. To a large extent it also reflects the contention between protecting professional plant breeders and smallholder farmers (Adebola 2019).

3.1. The Agreement on trade related aspects of intellectual property rights (TRIPS Agreement)

The TRIPS Agreement is a product of the Uruguay Round of the General Agreement on Tariff and Trade (GATT) held in 1994 under the auspices of the World Trade Organisation (WTO). It stipulates minimum standards of IP protection for all WTO Member States regarding the different categories of IPR frameworks, including patents. Nevertheless, it embraces flexibility as a cornerstone principle in recognition of the fact that a one-size-fits-all is untenable giving the different levels of development of the Member States (Musungu 2004). The relevant provisions for this article are Articles 8 and 27.

Article 8 states that Members may adopt measures consistent with the Treaty's provisions which are necessary to protect nutrition. Article 27(1) provides that 'patents shall be available for any inventions, whether products or processes, in all fields of technology, provided that they are new, involve an inventive step and are capable of industrial application'. But then Article 27(3)(b) provides:

> Members may also exclude from patentability – plants and animals other than microorganisms, and essentially biological processes for the production of plants or animals other than non-biological and microbiological processes. However, Members shall provide for the protection of plant varieties either by patents or by an effective sui generis system or by any combination thereof. p 60

In effect, section 27(3)(b) requires Member States to protect plant varieties either as patents, or PBRs or an effective *sui generis* system or a blend of the options. One of the important implications of the TRIPS Agreement is the liberty it grants members states to decide how to protect plant varieties and to opt for a *sui generis* framework (Helfer 2002). Still it leaves many uncertainties one of which is the non-clarification of what constitutes 'effective sui generis system' (Leskien and Flitner 1997; Tansey 2002).

3.2. International Convention for the Protection of New Varieties of Plants (UPOV Convention)

The UPOV Convention gets the price for the first international treaty bringing IP into agriculture. It was created in 1961 and entered into force in 1968, with the aim of harmonising and supporting national systems in Europe already operating commercial PBRs (Dutfield 2008, 27). It established the International Union for the Protection of New Varieties of Plants (Article 1(2) and Article 23 UPOV of the Convention 1978 and 1991 respectively) to help promote international harmonisation and assist countries to establish their PVP legislation. Since its inception, the UPOV Convention has undergone three revisions in 1972, 1978 and 1991, each one further strengthening its PBR system.

The Convention creates a binary system of rules for the protection of plant varieties by operating the 1978 framework alongside the stricter 1991 version, with some Members of the Union preferring the less rigid 1978 version which is suitable for countries that are 'net

Table 1. Major differences bewteen the provisions of the 1978 and 1991 UPOV Convention.

	1978	1991	Comments
Beneficiaries		**'Breeder' means:** a person who bred, or discovered and developed a variety, the employer of an inventor or one who commissioned the work subject to national law, and – successors-in-title of the 'breeder' so defined (Ar.1(4)).	**In effect, this provision extends the breeders' right to mere discoveries.**
Protectable subject matter	National law to determine (Articles 2(2) and 4)	Extends protection to all plant genera and species (Article 3)	The 1991 version adopts a rigid one-size-fits-all approach
Form of protection	States may protect plant varieties either as a sui generis law or as patent, but not both (Article 2(1))	'Each Contracting Party shall grant and protect breeders' rights' (Article 2)	The 1991 version's silence on patent technically allows double protection of plant varieties both as PBRs and patent.
Breeders' Right	Right to – produce for purposes of commercial marketing – offer for sale, and – market the reproductive or vegetative propagating material, as such, the variety (Article 5)	Production or reproduction, conditioning for the purpose of propagation, offering for sale, marketing, exporting, importing, stocking for any of the above purposes Art 14(1)	The 1991 version extends the scope of breeders' rights in the number of prohibited acts It also extends protection harvested materials obtained through unauthorised use of protected materials (Art. 14 (2)).
Exceptions	Largely allows states to determine the scope of breeders' rights and the exceptions.	Private use; non-commercial use, experimental use; use for further breeding (Article 15(1))	Creates mandatory as well as an optional exception for farmer's use of protected material
Breeder's Access right	Breeder's authorisation not required to create other varieties subject to certain conditions (Article 5(3))	Mandatory (Article 15(1)(ii) (iii))	
Farmer's privilege	Silent	Optional (Article 15(2))	Thus in both versions it is up to national law.
Specific section for exceptions	None	Article 15	1978 version: states have discretion to determine exceptions.

importers of plant varieties' and would prefer a shorter term of protection and more use of purchased seeds by farmers (Medaglia et al. 2019, 13). However, new members of the Union are mostly required to adopt the 1991 (Dutfield 2008, 32), while non-members can use the 1978 version if they so desired.

There are marked differences between the 1978 and 1991 UPOV versions as shown in Table 1 which have implications for food security.

The criteria for protection in both versions are similar although the terminologies differ (Article 6, 1978; Article 5, 1991). Basically, to qualify for protection under the UPOV system, the plant variety must be new, distinct, stable and uniform (homogenous). But the standard novelty refers to 'commercial novelty' (Dutfield 2008, 35), meaning the variety has not been presented in the market with the agreement of the 'breeder' (Article 6(1)(a) 1978 version; Article 6 1992 version).

The main problem with the 1991 UPOV which is not the case with the 1978 version is the creation of a broader scope of the PBR as contained in Article 14(1) without equal recognition of farmers' privilege. It further extends breeders' exclusive rights to harvest (Table 1). Hence, breeders can license others to produce their varieties but reserve to themselves the right to sell, exchange or export the product. This excludes farmers from selling their harvested materials unless authorised by the breeder. It also makes it possible for plant breeders to protect their species both as PVP and patents by not expressly prohibiting it (Medaglia et al. 2019, 13). Moreover, the reserved farmers' privilege as an exception to the breeders' right only applies to harvests from protected material planted 'on their own holdings' (Article 15(2)). Therefore, farmers cannot replant seeds of protected varieties received from others, which then restricts farmers from exchanging seeds within their community. The 1991 UPOV is also seen as overreaching by extending protection to discoveries as opposed to patent law, which generally does not protect mere discoveries (Dutfield 2008, 34).

3.3. Major issues with these frameworks for Nigeria's food self-sufficiency

Clearly, the treaties discussed above point to major issues that could have serious implications for the objective of food self-sufficiency and invariably food security. Central to these issues is the fact that smallholder farmers contribute significantly to food supply in African communities, by relying mostly on their traditional agricultural knowledge and practices. As such, any factor that affects smallholder farmers potentially affects food self-sufficiency.

Given the largely informal, open and collaborative nature of the African agricultural ecosystem, the concept of private monopolies that shape most current international IPR systems on agricultural resources seem unsuitable for Africa. Over 90% of all technology and product patents are under the control of developed countries (GRAIN 1998, 101), and proprietary biotechnologies are concentrated in a few transnational corporations (Blakeney 2009, 211). This signals potential access barriers to much needed IPR protected and dependency on foreign technology (AIA/GRAIN 1998; Adebola 2019). Kenya and South Africa who both have PBP laws are already exhibiting symptoms of this threat. It is reported that a larger proportion of farming seeds (90% and 60% irrespectively) are imported (Blakeney 2009).

The fundamental problem with the UPOV, particularly the more rigid 1991 version, is the patent-type system it implements which is more appropriate for countries with predominantly commercial and industrial agricultural. The UPOV system could create additional costs in royalties for the smallholders who may not be able to afford them consistently. The 1991 UPOV system may have allowed replanting but only on own holdings. It has been argued that this restricts farmers' freedom to buy seed from sources other than the original breeder. And for farmers who do not have alternative sources of income, preventing them from selling and exchanging their harvest threatens their livelihood and the objective of self-sufficiency (Ragavan and O'Shields 2007).

The separation of the roles of farming and plant breeding following the UPOV model contrasts with the predominant practice among farmers in Africa for whom plant breeding and farming are inseparable. This could disrupt the indigenous farming system in place. This constitutes great threat to Africa's long term food security and self-sufficiency since the 'rural majority are dependent for their food, medicine and shelter on the free access to and exchange of biological materials, knowledge, innovations and practices' (Ekpere 2000, 9). It also threatens the traditional role of farmers in developing and conserving biodiversity.

Also, the larger focus on plant breeders' right by the international frameworks creates an imbalanced system that does not instil trust in an ecosystem dominated by these same smallholders whose interests the system overlooks. Moreover, the conditions for the grant of both patents and breeder's rights are usually not realisable by smallholder farmers with regards to their own breeds. Indeed, it has been argued that the systems encourage bio-piracy and constitute a process of double theft. Developed countries 'steal' the innovations of local communities by claiming collective innovations, and then rob the community of the economic benefits derived from such products (Ekpere 2000, 3).

Furthermore, the TRIPS Agreement and the UPOV are in direct conflict with the basic tenets of the CBD which recognises the role and achievement of local and indigenous communities in the conservation of biodiversity as justification for the reaffirmation and protection of community rights (Ekpere 1999).

African countries are also worried that investments in plant breeding in the local seed industry tend to focus on a few varieties with global economic value leaving out a vast majority of the lesser known food crops (and traditional land races) in Africa (Oguamanam 2015, 176–186).

There are also environmental and health concerns arising from the patent and UPOV frameworks. They breed homogeneity and encourage GMOs whose health quality or effects are still under contention. Moreover, the cultivation of proprietary seeds alongside indigenous varieties (landraces) are said to harm the landraces overtime (Oguamanam 2015; Dutfield 2008, 41), points to dangers in encouraging widespread planting of genetically modified homogenous seeds as seen in the 1970 corn crisis which saw 15 per cent of the corn crop in that year 'lost to an epidemic of southern corn leaf blight' leading to a 20 percent rise in corn prices.

On the whole, the implementation of the TRIPS Agreement and the UPOV could create dependency instead of self-sufficiency in food production and supply for African countries, including Nigeria. Given the promises and perils effects of IPRs arising from the binary of interests, the more realistic approach is a balanced system that recognises farmer's rights alongside breeders' rights in recognition of their respective contributions to sustainable agriculture and food self-sufficiency.

3.4. The Convention on Biological Diversity (CBD)

The CBD was signed in 1992 and entered into force in 1993 against a background of increasing discontent of developing countries with the misappropriation of their genetic resources and the lop-sidedness of the global IPR system. It was essentially a pushback from developing countries against a system which failed to acknowledge or reward the contribution of their farmers whose knowledge often formed the basis of patented or PVP-protected innovations. There was also concern about the conservation of biodiversity (Tansey 2004, 264, 2008, 4–25).

Thus the overall objective of the CBD is the conservation of biodiversity based on sustainable use and to encourage a reward system to incentivise sustainable use and conservation in situ.

Article 3 of the CBD recognises the sovereignty of states over their resources including their genetic resources. However, Parties are to 'facilitate access to genetic resources for environmentally sound uses' Article 15(3). To achieve its objectives, it incorporates three basic principles that countries must heed to: namely, the conservation of biological diversity, the sustainable use of its components and the fair and equitable sharing of the benefits arising from the use of genetic resources (Article 15(5)). Sustainable use entailed recognising the role of local people living amid biodiversity and mobilising support for conservation through benefits (Article 8(j)) (Bragdon, Garforth, and Haapala 2008). It also requires the diffusion of such knowledge in an inclusive manner with benefits to all involve (Article 15(7)). Under the CBD, parties undertake to provide and/or facilitate access and transfer of technologies, including biotechnology, to other parties under fair and most favourable terms (16(1)(2)). The terms of access must be such that recognises 'and are consistent with the adequate and effective protection of intellectual property rights' (Article 16(2)).

3.5. International treaty on plant genetic resources for food and agriculture (ITPGRFA), 1983

The ITPGRFA was the culmination of a protracted campaign mainly driven by developing countries and their public interest NGOs to protect farmers' right as of right (Halewood and Nnadozie 2008, 119–120). But like the CBD, it was also recognised as a way of rewarding farmers and their communities for their past and present contributions to the world's reservoir of biodiversity and encouraging them further in conserving biodiversity. Article 1 establishes its objectives as conservation and sustainable use of PGRFA and fair and equitable sharing of benefits arising from their use, in harmony with the CBD, for sustainable agriculture and food security (Halewood and Nnadozie 2008, 129).

The ITPGRFA defines farmers' rights as 'rights arising from the past, present and future contribution of farmers in conserving, improving and making available plant genetic resources, particularly those in centres of origin/diversity.' The rights are vested in the International Community as trustee for present and future generations of farmers, for the purpose of ensuring full benefits to farmers, and supporting the continuation of their contributions (Annex II, Resolution 5/89 adopted by the FAO). Nations can decide how to protect farmers' rights and could choose to combine one of the versions of UPOV with some of the access principles of the CBD. Article 10 recognises the sovereign rights of States over their own PGRFA, and places the authority to determine access to those resources on national governments and national law.

The inclusion of farmers' rights in the Treaty marked the first time that such rights were formally recognised in an international instrument. However, developing a conceptual framework for the protection of the right is left to the state. This is probably in recognition that states can achieve this through a sui generis framework.

3.6. The African sui generis model

The African Model Law for the Protection of the Rights of Local Communities, Farmers and Breeders, and for the Regulation of Access to Biological Resources is an important template guiding the protection of farmers in Africa. Like the ITPGRFA, it emphasises the interests of farmers alongside breeders. It is guided by principles with focus on ensuring food security for the African context. It inaugurates a guide for OAU Member States (now the African Union) desirous of establishing a national legislation consistent with their needs, developmental level, and the dynamics of the African Agricultural ecosystem (Ekpere 2000). Thus it embraces core principles which are fundamental to the boosting of African food security networks and indigenous agriculture, such as, detachment of seeds from the bondage of private rights to keep seed free, community rights and responsibilities, recognition of the value of Indigenous Knowledge, full participation in decision making, access to biological and genetic diversity, prior informed consent, fair and equitable sharing of benefits, plant breeders rights, farmers' rights and zero patents on life forms (Preamble to the African Model Law).

The OAU's Model Law embraces the CBD. It governs access based on informed consent, benefit-sharing and community rights, including farmers' rights, as appropriate for Africa's peculiar characteristics of enormous biological and cultural diversity in dominantly rural societies. It rejects the UPOV Convention of 1991 as a *sui generis* model for plant varieties, as well as the patenting of micro-organisms which is seen as a tool for allowing foreign monopolies over African local biodiversity.

It recognises the rights of breeders over the varieties they develop, while promoting commercial plant breeding adapted to Africa's farming systems. While recognising and providing support for plant breeders' rights, the terms of protection are formulated in a way that does not undermine Africa's long tradition of community innovation and breeding through the new norms of commercial breeding and innovation. Its conception of breeders' rights aims to ensure that exclusively commercial breeders do not impinge on customary practices of farmers (Articles 24, 25 and 26) ... The plant breeder gets the exclusive rights to produce and sell the new variety developed (Articles 28 and 30). Conversely, farmers can save, use, exchange and sell farm-saved seed and other planting material. They can also use protected new varieties to develop their own farmers' varieties (Articles 31 and 33).

4. The Nigerian legal framework

Having noted the weaknesses of the international framework with potential threats to food self-sufficiency in Nigeria, and the terms of the ITPGFA and the African Model Law aimed at resolving some of the weaknesses, this section interrogates the Nigerian framework's support for the country's food sufficiency prospects.

4.1. The plant variety protection Act 2012

Nigeria's newly enacted PVP Act has generated mixed reactions among experts and concerned stakeholders (Plac Bills Track 2021; NESG 2021; Onyeji 2019). Some consider it necessary in unlocking all potential across the Nigerian agricultural ecosystem and transforming agriculture in Nigeria to meet the nutritional needs of the growing population, projected to hit 100 million by 2050 (Food Farm News 2019). But many are unimpressed; especially with the UPOV 1991 approach it adopted (NESG 2021; Adebola 2020). Like other African countries, Nigeria's move towards implementing a PVP framework was primarily inspired by the need to fulfil its obligations as a member of the WTO to install a national PVP system. Nevertheless, local demand for a PVP system also exists to accommodate the interests of the growing private seed sector, and encourage the development of local capacity in the aggrotech sector. Farmers suffer poor harvests which are attributed to the use of poor quality seeds, while piracy of proprietary seeds affects cooperate seed breeders in Nigeria and discourage investments (NESG 2021). A PVP system is seen as an answer to these challenges (NESG 2021).

The PVP Act aims to:

(a) promote increased staple crop productivity for smallholder farmers in Nigeria and encourage investment in plant breeding and crop variety development; (b) promote increased mutual accountability in the seed sector; and (c) protect new varieties of plants (section 1).

The Act applies to breeders, and any other genera and species (section 2). A breeder under the Act refers to: persons who bred or discovered and developed a variety; persons who employ the breeder or discoverer of the variety, and successors-in-title of these persons (Section 58). The Act covers all plant genera and species (section 12) satisfying the required criteria for protection, namely: newness, distinctiveness, uniformity and stability (section 13(a)). These requirements are identical with the 1991 version of the UPOV Convention (section 14, 15 and 16). They are the only accepted conditions for the grant of a breeder's right within section 13(2).

Section 30(1) delineates the scope of the breeder's right recalling the terms of the 1991 UPOV verbatim. Like the UPOV, it extends protection to harvested materials (section 30 (3)(a)(b)) and 'essentially derived' varieties (section 30(3)). Exceptions to the breeder's right are contained in section 31(1) again replicating the UPOV Convention. Exemptions are made for private and non-commercial use, research and further breeding. The breeder's exception and farmer's privilege also follow the UPOV 1991 standard.

Protection is for a minimum of 20 years and 25 for trees and vines. Section 59 criminalises the violation of a breeder's right.

By adopting the 1991 UPOV version, the PVP Act also considerably inherits its weaknesses especially those pertaining to the farmer's rights, the extension of PVP to discoveries and the extensive rights given to breeders to control harvests. Like the 1991 UPOV, the farmers' privilege only allows on-farm replanting but not seed sharing. Therefore, Nigerian farmers are not allowed their habitual practice of seed sharing within their community.

While it is envisaged that the Act would assist smallholder farmers to access affordable quality seeds, there is hardly any empirical study to backup this expectation. Instead evidence from other African countries currently operating similar UPOV modelled systems shows that smallholder farmers have not really benefited because it focuses more on commercially viable crops.

4.2. The national agricultural Seed Act 2019

The primary role of the Seed Act is regulation through certification (section 49), registration and labelling (section 35), monitoring and management. It provides support for the PVP system by regulating quality standards within Nigeria's seed section. Section 49 (1) provides '... any person who sells, keeps for sale, barters or otherwise supplies any seed of any variety or hybrid shall apply to the council for grant of certification for the purpose ... ' In other words, no seeds shall be commercialised in Nigeria without certification by the approved certification body.

Sections 39 enable the provision of temporary measures to protect breeder's rights. It empowers the Ministry of Agriculture to approve separate PVP legislation to support plant variety development.

The Seed Act was recently amended in response to current trends in global seed. One of the key changes is an increase in penalties (section 42). It is not clear what conflicts may arise between the Seed Act and the PVP Act, especially in view of section 13(2) of the PVP Act which ousts any extraneous conditions for the protection of plant varieties in Nigeria.

Hopefully, the Seed Act will not suffer the fate of the National Agricultural Seeds Decree, No.72 of 1992, which was never fully implemented because of the absence of the regulation that was to accompany the Decree.

4.3. The patent and designs Act (PDA)

The PDA, enacted in 1970, is below international standards, considering that since its inception, it has not been reviewed. The Industrial Property Commission Bill (IPCOM) seeking to amend and harmonised IP laws in Nigeria, including patent law is yet to be passed into law (Aluko and Oyebode 2020). Consequently, the standard of patent protection established by the PDA has been found 'unfit for purpose' (Mgbeoji 2014). As Mgbeoji argued, the system allows dubious applications for patent by foreigners to be granted. Oyewunmi observed that the Act established more of a patent registration than an examination system and patents are without confirmation of their validity in substance (Oyewunmi 2015). Section 1 provides, *inter alia*, that a patentable invention must be new, results from inventive activity and is capable of industrial application (Akpambang, 83).

Most importantly, the Act expressly prohibits the patenting of plant varieties. Section 1 (4)(a) provides that patent protection does not extend to 'plant or animal varieties, or essentially biological processes for the production of plants or animals (other than microbiological processes and their products)'. This forecloses the relevance of the Act to PVP in Nigeria.

Other governing legislations include the National Crop Varieties and Livestock Breeds (NCVLBA) (Registration etc.) Act, No.33 of 1987; the National Biosafety Management Agency Act of 2015 (1992 NASA); (Replaced by the National Biosafety Management Agency (Amendment) Act of 2019), the Agriculture (Control of Importation) Act of 1964; 2016 Guidelines for Registration and Release of New Crop Varieties in Nigeria 2016 (NACCGRAB), and the 2017 NASC Guidelines for Registration of Seed Producers or Companies and Seed Fields in Nigeria. While these are all connected to the seed sector, they do not confer private rights to plant varieties or privileges to farmers within the context IPR. They mainly help in regulating the commercial seed market.

5. Conclusion and recommendations

This article set out to determine whether the Nigerian framework supports agriculture in Nigeria as the starting point of becoming food self-sufficient; and if not, how the weaknesses can be addressed. The international patent and PVP systems built on the foundation of private rights and monopoly control have several implications, which, as this article has established, could inhibit agriculture in Nigeria. The shaping of Nigeria's laws on protecting agricultural inputs along these international frameworks without also being guided by the ITPGRFA, the CBD and the African Model Law, is a wrong approach because it imports many of the weaknesses of TRIPS and the UPOV frameworks.

No doubt, there is need to transform agriculture in Nigeria not only to address the collective needs of the different stakeholders, but also the food needs of a rapidly growing population. The extant framework does not holistically address these different interests in the Nigerian agricultural ecosystem. The appropriate framework requires a balanced approach that integrates the formal and informal agricultural sector, in recognition of the growing opportunities in the formal seed sector and the age-long contribution of smallholder farmers to agriculture in Nigeria, as equal partners in feeding the nation. The greater impetus given to breeder's right in the PVP Act relative to farmers' rights fosters an imbalance system and threatens the stability of the Nigerian agricultural farming system. The recommended option for Nigeria is a customised system that properly integrates these divergent interests guided by the African model and not the rigid UPOV model, designed for European countries. Such contextualised approach is permitted under Article 27(3) of TRIPS. Indeed, it has been recommended that developing countries are better off enacting a sui generis PVP legislation that would address their primary interests (CIPR 2002, 66). India heeded to this advice by shunning the UPOV system in favour of a specialised Indian-made system that evinces a genuine concern for farmers' right.

Finally, it must be emphasised that for the IPR system to succeed, a holistic approach is required to address other factors that impact food availability and affordability in Nigeria, such as conflicts, gender inequalities, particularly in the area of land ownership and access to agro aid programmes, increasing poverty, unemployment, environmental degradation, climate change, etc.

Disclosure statement

No potential conflict of interest was reported by the author(s).

References

Aday, Serpil, and Mehmet Seckin Aday. 2020. "Impact of COVID-19 on the Food Supply Chain." *Food Quality and Safety* 4 (4): 167–180. doi:10.1093/fqsafe/fyaa024.

Adebola, T. 2018. "Examining Plant Variety Protection in Nigeria: Realities, Obligations and Prospects." *The Journal of World Intellectual Property* 22 (1-2): 36–58.

Adebola, T. 2019. "Breaking the Silence on Patent Variety in Nigeria." FLORA IP, April 20.

Adebola, T. 2020. "Can the Subaltern Speak? Nigeria's untoward Path to UPOV, Flora IP, April.

Adebowale, N. 2020. "Nigeria COVID-19 – Nigeria's Third Phase of Eased Lockdown to Last Four Weeks."

Agency Report. 2017. "World Food Price: Africa Spends $35Billion Annually on Food Imports-Adesina." *Premium Times*, October 17. https://www.premiumtimesng.com/news/more-news/246415-world-food-prize-africa-spends-35bn-annually-food-imports-adesina.html.

AIA/GRAIN. 1998. "Ten Reasons not to Join UPOV, Global Trade and Biodiversity in Conflict." May 15. https://www.grain.org/article/entries/1-ten-reasons-not-to-join-upov.

Akpambang, Enobong Mbang. "An Evaluation of Legal Protection of New Plant and Animal Varieties Under Intel-lectual Property Law." Benson Idahosa University Journal of Private and Property Law.

Aluko and Oyebode. 2020. "The Pending Industrial Property Bill (IPCOM)." 2 *Intellectual Property Newsletter*. https://www.aluko-oyebode.com/insights/intellectual-property-newsletter-second-issue-2020/. The Bill seeks to harmonise all current IP laws, including the patent, plant varieties, animal breeders and farmers rights.

Anderson, R. 2005. "The History of Farmers' Rights: A Guide to Central Documents and Literature." The Fridtjof Nansen Institute Background Study 1, The Farmers' Rights Project, FNI Report 8/ 2005. http://www.fni.no/getfile.php/131903-1469869845/Filer/Publikasjoner/FNI-R0805.pdf.

ASM (American Society of Microbiology). 2020. "Supply Shortages Impacting COVID-19 and Non-COVID Testing." November 9. https://asm.org/Articles/2020/September/Clinical-Microbiology-Supply-Shortage-Collecti-1.

Baer-Nawrocka, A. , and A. Sadowski. 2019. "Food Security and Food Self-sufficiency Around the World: A Typology of Countries." *Plos ONE* 14 (3): e0213448.

Bakare, Adedayo. 2018. "Nigeria Needs Food Security, Not Food Self-Sufficiency." *Stears Business*, November 16. https://www.stearsng.com/article/nigeria-needs-food-security-not-food-self-sufficiency.

Blakeney, Michael. 2009. *Intellectual Property Rights and Food Security*. Wallington, Oxford: CABI.

Bragdon, Susan H., Kathryn Garforth, and John E. Haapala. 2008. "Safeguarding Biodiversity: The Convention on Biological Diversity." In *The Future Control of Food: A Guide to International Negotiations and Rules on Intellectual Property, Biodiversity and Food Security*, edited by Geoff Tansey and Tasmin Rajotte, 82–114. London: Routledge.

CIPR (Commission on Intellectual Property Rights). 2002. http://www.iprcommission.org.

Clapp, Jennifer. 2017. "Food Self-sufficiency: Making Sense of It, and When It Makes Sense." *Food Policy* 66: 88–96.

Dutfield, Graham. 2008. "Turning Plant Varieties into Intellectual Property: The UPO Convention." In *The Future Control of Food A Guide to International Negotiations and Rules on Intellectual Property, Biodiversity and Food Security*, edited by Geoff Tansey, and Tasmin Rajotte, 27–47. London: Routledge.

Ekpere, J. A. 1999. "Alternative to UPOV for the Protection of New Plant Varieties." May 17, GRAIN "Africa's alternative to UPOV".

Ekpere, J. A. 2000. "The OAU's Model Law: The Protection of the Rights of Local Communities, Farmers and Breeders, and for the Regulation of Access to Biological Resources." An Explanatory Booklet. https://www.blauen-institut.ch/s2_blue/tx_blu/tp/tpt/t_oau_model_law.pdf.

FAO. 1999. *Implications of Economic Policy for Food Security: A Training Manual*. http://www.fao.org/ 3/x3936e/x3936e03.htm.

FAO. 2015–16. "Food Self-sufficiency and International Trade: A False Dichotomy?" http://www.fao. org/3/i5222e/i5222e.pdf.

FAO. 2017. The State of Food and Agriculture: Leveraging Food Systems for Inclusive Rural Transformation. http://www.fao.org/3/a-I7658e.pdf.

FAO, IFAD and WFP. 2013. *The State of Food Insecurity in the World: The Multiple Dimensions of Food Security*. Rome: FAO. https://www.fao.org/3/i3434e/i3434e.pdf.

FMARD (Federal Ministry of Agriculture and Rural Development). 2016. "The Agriculture Promotion Policy 2016 - 2020." http://nssp.ifpri.info/files/2017/12/2016-Nigeria-Agric-Sector-Policy-Roadmap_June-15-2016_Final.pdf.

Food Farm News. 2019. "Plant Variety Protection Law Will Boost Food Security-DG Seeds Council." November 6. Independent. Tuesday November 12.

GAIN. 2020. "Impact of COVID-19 on Food Systems: A Situation Report" 2nd ed. April 22, p 6.

Gollin, Michael A. 2008. *Driving Innovation: Intellectual Property Strategies for a Dynamic World*. New York: Cambridge University Press.

Halewood, Michael, and Kent Nnadozie . 2008. "Giving Priority to the Common: The International Treaty on Plant Genetic Resources for Food and Agriculture." In *The Future of Food: A Guide to International Negotiations and Rules on Intellectual Property, Biodiversity and Food Security*, edited by Geoff Tansey and Tasmin Rajotte, 115–140. London: Routledge.

Haugen, H., M. R. Muller, and S. M. Narasimhan. 2010. "Food Security and Intellectual Property Rights: Finding the Linkages." In *Intellectual Property and Human Development: Current Trends and Future Scenarios*, edited by T. Wong, and G. Dutfield, 103–138. Cambridge: Cambridge University Press.

Helfer, Laurence R. 2002. Intellectual Property Rights in Plant Varieties: An Overview with Options for National Governments (2002), (FAO legal Papers Online # 31) at 31. Accessed April 20, 2021. http://www.fao.org/Legal/Prs-OL/lpo31.pdf.

Ibrahim, Ridwan Lanre, Kazim Bello Ajide, and Omokanmi Olatunde Julius. 2020. "Easing of Lockdown Measures in Nigeria: Implications for the Healthcare System." *Health Policy Technology* 9 (4): 399–404.

Kuhlmann, Karin, Yuan Zhou, Adron Nalinya Naggayi, and Heather Lui. 2018. "Seed Policy Harmonisation in ECOWAS: The Case of Nigeria." Working Paper NML.

Kuyek, Devlin. 2002. "Intellectual property Rights in African Agriculture: Implications for Small Farmers." GRAIN August.

Laborde, David, Will Martin, Johan Swinnen, and Rob Vos. 2020. "COVID-19 Risks to Global Food Security." *Science* 369 (6503): 500–502.

Leskien, Dan, and Michael Flitner. 1997. Intellectual Property Rights and Plant Genetic Resources: Options for a Sui Generis System (Issue in genetic Resources No. 6) at 26. Accessed May 5, 2021. http://www.bioviersityinternational.org/publications/pdf/497.pdf.

Mahmoud, Barakat. 2018. "Value-Added Products Reduce Food Loss and Strengthen Resilience, Food Security and Nutrition." *Agrilinks*, October 12.

Medaglia, J. C., C. Oguamanam, O. Rukundo, and F. Perron-Welch. 2019. "Comparative Study of the Nagoya Protocol, the Plant Treaty and the UPOV Convention: The Interface of Access and Benefit Sharing and Plant Variety Protection." Centre for International Sustainable Development Law (CISDL).

Merges, Robert P., P. S. Menell, and M. A. Lemley.2000. *Intellectual Property in the New Technological Age*. 2nd ed. Gaithersburg, MD: Aspen Law and Business.

Mgbeoji, Ikechi. 2014. "African Patent Offices Not Fit for Purpose." In *Innovation and Intellectual Property: Collaborative Dynamics in Africa*, edited by Jeremy de Beer, Chris Armstrong, Chidi Oguamanam, and Tobias Schonwetter, 234–247. Cape Town: UCT Press.

Minot, Nicholas, and Nidup Pelijor. 2010. "Food Security and Food Self-Sufficiency in Bhutan." International Food Policy Research Institute (IFPRI) Report. https://ifpri.org/publication-food-security-and-food-self-suffciency-bhutan.

Muredzi, P., and Emmanuel Sackey. 1995. *Food Security and Intellectual Property Rights - Lessons from Sub-Saharan Africa*. Lambert Academic Publishing.

Musungu, S. F., et al. 2004. "Utilizing Trips Flexibilities for Public Health Protection through South-South Regional Frameworks." South Centre. https://citeseerx.ist.psu.edu/viewdoc/download?doi=10.1.1.297.6970&rep=rep1&type=pdf.

NESG (Nigerian Economic Summit Group). 2021. "Experts Review of the Plant Variety Protection Bill." https://nesgroup.org/events/Experts-review-of-the-Plant-Variety-Protection-Bill,-Significance-and-Constraints.

Niada, Laura. 2006. "Hunger and International Law: The Far- Reaching Scope of the Human Right to Food." *Connecticut Journal of International Law* 22: 131, at 151.

Obonyilo, P. A. 2008. Global Food Crisis with Emphasis on Nigeria. Ripples from the Faith Magazine; An NFCS BUK Publication. https://www.slideshare.net/ObonyiloPaulAaron/global-food-crisis-with-emphasis-on-nigeria.

Oguamanam, Chidi. 2015. "Breeding Apples for Oranges: Africa's Misplaced Priority Over Plant Breeders' Rights." *The Journal of World Intellectual Property* 18 (5): 165–195.

O'Hagan, J. P. 1976. "National Self-Sufficiency in Food." *Food Policy* 1 (5): 355–366.

Onyeji, Ebuka. 2019. "Why Nigeria Should Develop Own Indigenous Plant Variety Protection Laws – Experts." Premium Times, April 16.

Osabohien, R. A., Evans Osabuohien, and Ese Urhie. 2017. "Food Security, Institutional Framework and Technology: Examining the Nexus in Nigeria Using ARDL Approach." *Current Nutrition & Food Science* 13 (4): 1–10.

Oyewunmi, Adejoke O. 2015. *Nigerian Law of Intellectual Property*. Lagos: University of Lagos Press and Bookshop.

Penrhys-Evan, Toby. 2020. "The Unintended Consequences of COVID19 Lockdown in Nigeria." Accessed September 10, 2020. http://www.future-agricultures.org/blog/the-unintended-consequences-of-COVID19-Lockdown-in-Nigeria.

Plac Bills Track. 2021. "HB 68: Plant Variety Protection (PVP) Bill, 2021." https://placbillstrack.org/view.php?getid=7942.

Punch. 2020. Editorial "Time to Mobilise for Food Self-sufficiency." June 2.

Ragavan, Srividhya, and Jamie Mayer O'Shields. 2007. "Has India Addressed its Farmers Woes? A Story of Plant Protection Issues." *Georgetown. International Environmental Law Review* 20: 97, at 98.

Rocca, Camilla, and Ines Schultes. 2020. "Food Insecurity in Africa: Deadlier than COVID-19?" Mo Ibrahim Foundation. https://mo.ibrahim.foundation/sites/default/files/2020-05/food-insecurity-in-africa_0.pdf.

Rome Declaration on World Food Security and World Food Summit Plan of Action. 1996. World Food Summit, 13–17 November, Rome Italy, Rome, FAO, 43 p. 9. http://www.fao.org/docrep/003/w3613e/w3613e00.htm.

Sahel. 2017. "Tomato Value Chain in Nigeria." *Sahel Newspaper*, Vol. 15, July 18, p. 1. http://www.fni.no/getfile.php/131903-1469869845/Filer/Publikasjoner/FNI-R0805.pdf.

Sahel Quarterly. 2021. Critical Trends in Agriculture and Food in Africa for the Next Decade, vol. 26, January. p. 27 https://sahelconsult.com/wp-content/uploads/2021/01/Sahel-Quarterly-_Critical-Trends-in-Agriculture-and-Food-in-Africa-for-the-Next-Decade-Volume-26.pdf.

Schlein, Lisa. 2020. "COVID-19 is Threatening Food Security in Nigeria." VOA, June 9. https://www.voanews.com/africa/covid-19-threatening-food-security-nigeria.

SDG. 2 to End Hunger Recognizes the Need to a Profound Change of the Global Food and Agriculture System. See SDG, SDG Goal 2: Zero hunger." https://www.un.org/sustainabledevelopment/hunger/.

Spore. 2017. "Agriculture Trade: Transforming the Informal Economy." *Spore Magazine*, November 30. https://www.mamopanel.org/news/in-the-news/2017/dec/4/agricultural-trade-transforming-informal-economy/.

State House. 2020. "President Buhari's Remarks at the National Food Security Council Meeting." September 19. https://nigerianembassy.nu/president-buharis-remarks-at-the-national-food-security-council-meeting/.

Tansey, G. 2002. *Food Security, Biotechnology and Intellectual Property: Unpacking Some Issues Around TRIPS*. Geneva: Quaker United Nations Office. www.quno.org/economicissues/intellectual-property/intellectualLinks.htm.

Tansey, Joef. 2004. "Global Intellectual Property Rights: A New Factor in Farming." In *Agriculture and the WTO: Creating a Trading System for Development*, edited by Merlinda Ingco, and John D. Nash, 253–268. Washington, DC: International Development Bank and Oxford Press.

Tansey, G. 2008. "Food, Farming and Global Rules." In *The Future Control of Food: A Guide to International Negotiations and Rules on Intellectual Property, Biodiversity and Food Security*, edited by Geoff Tansey and Tasmin Rajotte, 3–24. London: Routledge.

Thippeswamy, S. 2017. "Plant Variety Protection: An Historical Perspective." *International Journal of Development Research* 7 (11): 16839–16843.

Vaughan, Alan. 2019. "How Deadly Disease Outbreaks Could Worsen as the Climate Changes." *NewScientist*, October 15. https://www.newscientist.com/article/2219981-how-deadly-disease-outbreaks-could-worsen-as-the-climate-changes/#ixzz6ebZzLb1G.

WIPO. "What are Intellectual Property Rights?" https://www.wipo.int/about-ip/en/https://www.wto.org/english/tratop_e/trips_e/intel1_e.htm#:~:text=Intellectual%20property%20rights%20are%20the,a%20certain%20period%20of%20time.

WIPO. 2004. *Intellectual Property Handbook: Policy, Law and Use*. 2nd ed. Geneva: WIPO.

World Bank. 2021. "COVID 19 and Food Security." June 18. World Bank. https://www.worldbank.org/en/topic/agriculture/brief/food-security-and-covid-19.

Online learning during COVID19 and beyond: a human right based approach to internet access in Africa

Bukola Faturoti

ABSTRACT
Teaching and learning were disrupted due to lockdown imposed as part of efforts to curb the spread of the COVID19 virus that hit the world in 2020. As a result, many national governments requested educational establishments to migrate their teachings online. In Africa, internet penetration has improved in the last decade. However, the continent still lags in integrating the Internet into learning. Besides, there is unequal access to technologies used in online education and unequal access to data and connectivity. Regarding access to quality learning, the COVID-19 pandemic has widened the gap between the rich and the poor and has exposed society's fragility. This paper evaluates the strategies of African leaders in sustaining access to learning and the experience of learners during COVID19 lockdown. It argues that most African countries' educational systems are unprepared for the sudden switch to online learning. Finally, it investigates future policy strategies in bringing more Africans out of the digital desert.

Introduction

In 2020, COVID19 tested the resilience of the educational system. Almost 2 billion students, worldwide, had their studies disrupted due to schools' closure (UN 2020b). The closure of educational establishments at the height of the COVID19 pandemic could be resolved in two ways. First, teaching could be suspended until treatment is found COVID19. However, the impact of the indefinite suspension of studies would be far-reaching even outside the educational sector. Second, alternative teaching and learning methods would be needed to mitigate the effects of the pandemic on the educational system. The Internet and other communication technologies like television, radio have become veritable tools in this regard. Of the available technologies, the Internet is the most amenable in alleviating challenges posed to learning. First, it could deliver synchronous and asynchronous teaching. Second, Internet access enhances and facilitates students' engagement during learning, thereby assuming the status of transformative tool for education and training. Tellingly, "[w]hether textbooks will continue as a meaningful category of learning materials is itself put in question by developments enabled by the internet." (Rens 2020). Third, the Internet could be a gateway to educational resources for students in remote areas.

Access to the Internet enables a learner to participate more fully in their education and to develop skills essential to promoting their lifelong development and success. While COVID19 has deepened the role of technology as an enabler of education, it highlights the intra-digital divide within each country, both developing and developed countries alike. In the UK and Germany, learners in lower-earning households had no access to a laptop, desktop, or tablet and access to the Internet (Coleman 2021; Woessmann et al. 2020). Correspondingly, the lockdown brought to the fore the intra-African variability where some countries cannot afford or ignore the investment in digital learning infrastructure and platforms (OECD 2020). Although all Africa countries have legal provisions recognising the right to education, there is no corresponding law on access to the Internet. Policies relating to internet access operate in parallel rather than as a component of education provision. Outright lack or unequal access to the Internet could cause "black holes of information capitalism", resulting in further alienation of minority groups (Castells 2010).

Access to ICT infrastructure is crucial for achieving Sustainable Development Goals (SDGs). The 2030 Agenda for Sustainable Development calls for building " ... resilient infrastructure, promote sustainable industrialisation and foster innovation by 2030".[1] SDG Target 9c aims at: "significantly increase access to information and communications technology and strive to provide universal and affordable access to the internet in least developed countries by 2020".[2] Considering experience of learners in Africa during COVID19 lockdown, the 2020 target might have come a little too late. Africa will achieve its universal broadband objective when it brings 1.1billion residents of the continent online. This is an aspiration with a $100b price tag that will address the infrastructural deficiency, address the skills gap, and develop an appropriate regulatory framework (World Bank 2019). Universal Access and Service policies ensure the availability, affordability, and accessibility of communications services, including the Internet. Thus, the effectiveness of a country's "internet inclusion policy" is imperative when evaluating internet penetration in any country (Wentrup et al. 2016).

As of 10 March 2021, Africa had recorded 3,982,826 cases of COVID19 with 106,422 deaths. The continent reported its first COVID19 case on 14 February 2020 after a Chinese national who flew into Cairo tested positive for the virus. The first case in sub-Saharan Africa was reported in Lagos, Nigeria, on 28 February 2020 when an Italian businessman tested positive after arriving in the country. Like other continents, COVID19 poses a serious threat to the social dynamics, economic growth, and security of Africa. To combat its spread, commercial and religious activities were suspended while civil servants of lower grades had to work from home.[3] National governments directed educational establishments to stop physical activities and migrate their teaching to the virtual environment. Arguably, Africa has been very proactive in tackling the importation and intra-continent transmission of the COVID19. However, it is doubtful whether strategies to sustain access to education were effective.

This paper evaluates the experience of online learners vis-à-vis access to the Internet during COVID19. What are the prospects of online learning during and after COVID19 lockdown? Drawing from available data, Part II argues that the online learning experience was haphazard and catastrophic. Part III navigates the contour of internet access as a human right in the absence of clear-cut legal frameworks. Finally, Part IV evaluates initiatives for post COVID19 online and broadband access in general.

Part II learning during COVID19 in Africa: an evaluation

The national governments strategic responses for continuous delivery of education varied between Africa countries and educational sectors; nonetheless, some commonalities exist. For instance, most governments physical classes and took over the administration of teaching in public primary and secondary schools, but private school proprietors were given flexibility on their operation of remote teaching. Beyond requiring tertiary educational establishments to stop face-to-face teaching, there was no other intervention at this level of education. So, universities and colleges had independence in designing their strategies in sustaining learning.

The sudden migration into the virtual environment for many schools was hindered by challenges not limited to the skills gap, lack of planning and preparation for digital delivery and suitability of online platforms (Hodges et al. 2020). Research shows that in Africa, the use of the Internet for teaching and learning remains at the peripheral rather than an integral part of the educational process, especially at the secondary and the primary level of education (EdTeach Hub 2020). This is not significantly different at most public tertiary institutions where institutions are not obliged to provide internet access on the campus. Before the COVID19 outbreak, internet supply had been privately procured by students and academic staff to advance their research, while institutions with access were plagued with poor connectivity. Even where these institutions have virtual learning platforms, they are used variedly. Unlike government-owned institutions, privately owned educational establishments could transpose their teaching online with ease. Their facilities are designed with the contemplation of integrating modern technologies into academic activities. These institutions are profit-driven, and they charge exorbitant tuition fees.[4]

Use of TV and radio sets

Given the existential digital poverty on the continent, most governments resorted to radio sets and television technologies for the continued provision of teaching. Africa appears to be the most active in leveraging either TV or radio in filling the learning vacuum created by the lockdown (UNESCO 2020). The relatively ease of accessibility of TV or radio technology make them the preferred choice for many governments. For example, the Cote Devoire's Ministry of National Education collaborated with UNICEF to launch *Mon école à la Maison* (My School at Home) to provide educational lessons through television and radio broadcast for preschool, elementary, and middle school and high school students.[5] Similarly under the Ethiopian COVID-19 Education Sector Emergency Response Plan, the government provided radio lessons for primary school students and TV programmes for secondary school students in different regions (Yorke et al. 2020). The Association for the Development of Education in Africa (ADEA) curated strategic responses in Congo DRC, Rwanda, Ghana, Morocco, Mali and South Africa (ADEA 2020). Apparently, these technologies were deemed more suitable for pupils at pre-school age and primary school education. Countries that used both technologies were able to accommodate students with hearing and visual impairments. However, reliance on radio sets and printed materials alienated students who used sign language for communication.[6]

The impact and outcomes of this strategy are mixed. The durability of learning through the use of tv and radio during the pandemic is questionable. First, access to electricity either in urban or rural areas raises some concerns. Despite being a public good (Tully 2006), two-third of households do not have access to electricity in Africa (Brew-Hammond and Kemausuor 2009). While North Africa reached almost universal access to electricity by 2018, the electrification rate in sub-Saharan Africa was 45% in that year (International Energy Agency 2019).[7] Some countries suffer constant intermittent power supply while others rely on rationing to meet demands from growing populations (Soyemi et al. 2021). In urban areas of Nigeria, for example, most homes rely on generators to ameliorate the government's failure to provide stable electricity (Adewuyi et al. 2000). Aside from the exorbitant cost of fuel to power generators, students learning is disrupted anytime there is an outage and by noise.

Second, the adoption of tv and radio also raises complex pedagogical concerns. The sudden adoption of online learning has the potential to diminish the quality of teaching and student engagement (Hodges et al. 2020). Admittedly, learning becomes passive as students lack opportunities to seek clarification. Radio learners had to rely more on their imaginations, making this technology's suitability doubtful, especially for some subjects. Additionally, the organisations of classes are somewhat complicated. Many Ministries of Education are confused about the subjects to cover, the level to prioritise, the duration of classes, synchronisation of curriculum and inclusion of slow learners. Furthermore, there are no educational contents in audio-visual formats to cater for those with hearing impairment. Many countries had difficulties in producing content in quantity and quality in a short time; there were no pre-existing partnerships for the design and broadcasting of the educational content, and the lack of the know-how and expertise in monitoring and evaluation of learning (UNESCO 2020). Admittedly, using these technologies seems more like a box-ticking exercise as the content of materials is quite superficial and alienates many learners.

However, it is worth noting that the contribution of educational broadcasts through tv and radio surpasses the needs of students alone. For instance, some countries use these technologies to bridge the intergenerational learning gap. They are also used to educate the populace on safety protocol to prevent the transmission of COVID19 and other psychosocial well-being (UNESCO 2020).[8]

Internet and remote learning

Arguably, for the first time, learning via the Internet became a significant part of teaching and learning in Africa. However, the deployment and its success vary across African countries and levels of education. From the discussion above, it appears government strategies prefer using online learning methods for students at secondary and higher institutions. As such, less affluent pupils at the early childhood education level are disadvantaged due to the inefficiency of tv and radio technologies. When Rwanda provided zero-rated internet access to online platforms and zero fees for SMS, no provision was made for early childhood education learners in Ghana, Madagascar and DRC (ADEA).

(Davids 2020) argues that the closure of schools has given learners in private schools and affluent middle-class public schools extra edge over their colleagues in disadvantaged communities. These privileged learners have access to devices and connectivity but also support from teachers and parents. Conversely, their counterparts lack access to the Internet, and parents may be digitally illiterate to provide the needed support. As a result, the attrition rate among learners from economically poor communities may surge post COVID19 era (Le Grange 2020).

Although half of its population have access to the Internet, e-learning is still at its formative stage in Algeria. The country's e-learning platform BeeForm launched in November 2017 to provide companies and public institutions with digital tools for training on a mass level (Oxford Business Group 2018). In mitigating the disruption to learning, the Algerian Ministry of Education made available educational material on YouTube for students within the K12 sector (Redouane 2020). It also partnered with the country's National Office for Distance Learning and Training in providing access to a list of websites and electronic platforms deemed suitable for K12 students to assess on the Internet. At this level, the pedagogical practices are pretty rudimentary. Merely providing access to materials will not translate into learning without systematic teaching. Systematic teaching requires the input of a tutor who selects and arranges information in a manner that guarantee continuity and progression in learning. University students, on the other hand, were able to explore the existing e-learning platforms. Delivery of lectures moved online through platforms like Zoom, Google Hangouts, and Microsoft Teams. However, learners and their teachers had to contend with slow internet connection and a lack of ICT infrastructure for large scale emergency remote education. In some instances, classes were cancelled because several lecturers had technical difficulties, trouble with WiFi, or panicked over the prospect of teaching the full class over the new platform. A survey documented the experience of one of the teachers thus "Internet connection was so weak; I was obliged to wait for two days to upload a video of 4 mins!" (Hadjeris 2021). The President of the *Fédération Nationale des Associations de parents D'élèves* explained that.

> "With the coronavirus, we had to move quickly and implement distance learning. There are some courses online, but not everyone is lucky enough to have a computer or an internet connection. We have a lot of large families, and it is difficult for the children to find a quiet spot in the house. So, in our situation, distance learning with television is more democratic ... " (Zermane and Aitouche 2020)

Though the Internet could remedy some of the gaps of television and radio, this is hampered by internet access and connectivity.

The Democratic Republic of Congo (DRC) Instituted a nationwide lockdown on 19 March, forcing the closure of schools and universities across the country (Bigaba 2020). DRC's internet coverage is estimated to be less than 20%, and only 8% of households have internet access (ACAPS 2020). Average mobile phone penetration rates are only 26% compared to 43% in the region as a whole, and only 9% of individuals across the country use the Internet (GSMA 2015). Unlike primary school pupils who were taught through community radio stations under the partnership between education Cannot Wait, and UNESCO's Capacity Development for Education Programme, there was no respite for students in tertiary education. Most universities do not have reliable internet connectivity, and this requires the intervention of private operators. The problem is exacerbated where students have to study from home. A faculty member at the University of Kinshasa surmises that "Internet connection remains a luxury for Congolese students. How do you organise distance learning when many students don't have the necessary equipment to have online classes? ... They can have a computer, but don't have electricity or Internet. It's difficult at the moment to think of distance and online learning" (Nkashama 2020).

Turning to East Africa, as of 2020, with 43 million internet users, Kenya has the third-highest number of internet users in Africa, behind Nigeria and Egypt (Johnson 2021). Internet activities have increased considerably since the introduction of the mobile telephone network in the early 2000s. While many business firms were quick in their adoption, there was less enthusiasm for non-commercial purposes adoptions. With the advent of the mobile telephone, there was a dramatic upsurge in internet activities. Internet penetration rose from 0.3 per cent to 45 per cent in the period 2000–16. The growth rate of internet users increased from 99.9 per cent in 2001–149.3 per cent in 2006 but gradually declined to 3.7 per cent in 2016, reflecting increasing market saturation among households (Edo, Okodua, and Odebiyi 2019).

In ensuring internet access and continued learning, the Kenya Civil Aviation Authority (KCAA) entered into a partnership with Alphabet Inc. and Telkom Kenya to float Google's Loon Balloons carrying 4G base stations over Kenyan airspace.[9] In another collaboration, Safaricom, a private mobile network operator, and Eneza Education, Longhorn Publishers and Viusasa teamed up to support primary and secondary school students with free access to educational e-content. Eneza Education waived the daily subscription fee to its 'Shupavu291' platform for 60 days. As a result, learners could access up to 250MB of educational content, Viusasa E-learning and the Longhorn E-learning portal per day through the Safaricom network.

Substituting physical classes with online learning implicates contractual performance, especially variation in a contractual agreement. There is a perception of online learning being of lower quality than face-to-face learning (Inman, Kerwin, and Mayes 1999). Therefore, they should not be equally priced. The Kenyan court was asked to determine whether fee paying institutions could charge full tuition where they could not continue to provide face-to-face learning, which was within the contemplation of their contracts with parents and their wards. In *SPG (Suing as parents and guardians of students minors currently schooling at Sabis International School – Runda) v Directors, Sabis International School - Runda & 3 others,*[10] the petitioner had asked the court order that they did not have to pay full fees for the third term or until the Minister of Education reopens schools, whichever is the later. The parents argued that COVID19 had altered the contract signed with the school to provide accommodation, boarding facilities, access to an auditorium, a library and a laboratory. While the school agreed that its position of the contract had been altered, it contended that this was a private matter over which the court had no jurisdiction. The court rejected the respondent's argument and granted the interim order staying implementation of payment of full fees and allowed the Petitioners to offset up to and 80% for term 3.[11]

The private-public partnership between the Kenya Government and telecommunication service providers could not prevent the digital alienation of rural resident learners in Kenya caused by poor connectivity and lack of access to electricity (Parsitau and Jepkemei 2020). Besides, interoperability and compatibility become another obstacle in these communities. Navigating internet access involves complex negotiations. Many learners do not have smartphones and other ICT facilities. The competition for smartphones means that some children will have limited or no access to learning. Where adults have smartphones, there are tensions around privacy and kids' unsupervised internet access. Moreover, where electricity and technology do exist, the cost of the Internet is prohibitive. As a result, rural learners are put in a precarious position during national examinations.

In summary, the adoption of the Internet and allied digital platforms for learning during COVID19 lockdown is a cataclysmic failure. The Human Rights Watch documents typologies of learning experiences during the lockdown (Human Rights Watch 2020). First, some pupils were outrightly alienated from learning. For example, a mother in North Kivu, Congo, lamented, "It does not make me happy that my children are no longer going to school. Years don't wait for them. They have already lost a lot. What will become of our uneducated children?" Second, some students were lucky to have access to some form of learning but did through many struggles. In South Africa, a 17-year-old student complained about her ability to study effectively with online tools (Human Rights Watch 2020). Some students had to resort to rationing of internet data by prioritising which subject to download online (Human Rights Watch 2020). Another student had to use his mother's phone to do research on Google and YouTube when his school provided no form of learning. These narratives resonate in West Africa, where some parents complained of limited or expensive internet access.[12] Third, some pupils had no form of classes. In Morocco, some teachers did not turn up for their classes due to the inability to procure internet data (Human Rights Watch 2020). Finally, tutors are also victims just like their pupils. Apart from outright lack or unstable connectivity, some teachers are ill-equipped for the intrigues of online learning and integration of technologies into their teaching (ADEA 2020).

Indubitably, the African education sector is quite diverse, and its challenges vary. First, the worst-hit are the children of primary school education who are ostracised by the strategic responses of governments. Unlike their counterparts in the developed world, who are "digital natives", they do not have adequate formal education at home or access to Internet-enabled devices. For this group of learners, their problems are not just about access to quality and speed of the Internet but lack of devices for learning. Second, most responses are reactionary. Many schools and governments are not prepared for the closure and the subsequent migration of studies online. The adoption of online learning was a political decision without the understanding that technology enabled education is a long-term project with a commensurate investment. While the inability to foresee the COVID19 pandemic might be pardonable, the lack of political foresight is not. Disappointedly, national policies have not been prepared to support digital access and digital literacy. Many governments neglect to initiate or implement policies or laws requiring ISPs to extend their services to public institutions like schools, libraries, and the remote areas of their country. As it will later be argued below, universal access and universal services failed. The partnerships with telecoms companies are not far-reaching. Third, internet accessibility and affordability are two sides of the same coin; and their absence poses a threat to effective learning. Where available, the connectivity is weak to support synchronous and interactive teaching (Le-Grange 2004).

Part III international law and right of Internet access

Lack of internet access, data devices and digital skill gaps aggravate digital inequality. According to (Steele 2019),

> [d]igital inequality is evident between communities living in urban areas and those living in rural settlements; between socioeconomic groups; between less economically developed countries and more economically developed countries; between the educated and uneducated population. Individuals with access to a broadband connection can be digitally split. How? Low-performance computers limited broadband speeds and limited access to subscription-based content widen the gap.

Even where there is access, the socio-economic ability prevents people in Africa from appropriating the Internet.

Many African countries' sudden turn to technology at the peak of the COVID19 crisis portrays an instrumentalist perspective of technology. According to this construct, "technologies are 'tools' standing ready to serve the purposes of users." (Feenberg 1991). Given its neutrality, a technological device is evaluated on the basis of the particular employments that have been decided by its human designer or user (Gunkel 2020). However, this approach ignores the embodied and socially embedded nature of individual learners. An instrumentalist approach to the use of technology for educational purposes treats digital technology as a mere tool to be given to everybody to be equally accepted and effectively used (du Toit and Verhoef 2018). This digital divide is 'constructed socio-economically rather than generationally, with users from privileged backgrounds tending to use the Internet more widely and effectively than their less privileged peers' (du Toit and Verhoef 2018). This is in contradistinction to an embodied understanding of technology. Here, there is an emphasis on the interaction of students with technology. This perspective of technology recognises the student's personhood considering characteristics such as language, culture, perceptual faith and imagination. It allows the transition and systemic development and how learners evolve with their learning process.

The Internet has contributed to the removal of cultural, economic and geographical barrier to communication. Internet access is linked to other rights like freedom of expression, freedom of assembly and access to education. The right to education is also crucial to actualising other economic, social and political rights (Coccoli 2017; Faturoti 2021). Thus, the Internet has acquired a centripetal power to which all other rights gravitate; this new power has sparked a debate whether it should be elevated to the status of (human) right.[13]

Crucial to the recognition of internet access as a human right is the existence of a robust normative framework in the form of international human rights law advocating such rights. Due to its relative novelty, human rights to access the Internet have not found support under any international law. Creating a new human right is a tedious process requiring the consensus of academic scholars, civil societies, human rights stakeholders, and national governments.

The UN might be termed prophetic, two decades before the COVID19 pandemic, when in its Millennium Declaration resolved to ensure that the benefits of new technologies - information and communication technologies are available to all (United Nations 2000b). Also, the World Summit on Information Society (WSIS) states that "ICTs should be regarded as tools and not as an end in themselves" (ITU 2003). Their significance means that that "Everyone, everywhere should have the opportunity to participate and no one should be excluded from the benefits the Information Society offers" (ITU 2003). Though WSIS fails to declare Internet access a human right, it advocates for universal ICT access. Ordinarily, universal, ubiquitous, equitable, and affordable access to ICT infrastructure and services is absent. This challenge can only be overcome by the national government in collaboration with other stakeholders such as the private sector, civil society, and other international bodies responsible for developing the Information Society (ITU 2003).

La Rue, the Special Rapporteur on the Promotion and Protection of the right to freedom of opinion and expression for the United Nations (UN), concludes that States should prioritise universal access to the Internet through concrete and effective policy (LaRue 2011). His report submits that there are bases under international law to treat internet access as a human right:

> By explicitly providing that everyone has the right to express him or herself through any media, the Special Rapporteur underscores that article 19 of the Universal Declaration of Human Rights and the Covenant was drafted with foresight to include and to accommodate future technological developments through which individuals can exercise their right to freedom of expression. Hence, the framework of international human rights law remains relevant today and equally applicable to new communication technologies such as the Internet. (LaRue 2011)

Be that as it may, Art 19 does not expressly proclaim internet access as a human right; instead, it recognises the sameness of human rights online and offline. Even where it does, UDHR is not a binding treaty. However, the provision of UDHR is *imperi materia* with Art 19 of the International Covenant on Civil and Political Rights (ICCPR). Although the Human Rights Committee is short in declaring that internet access is a human right, it underscores the need of State parties to take cognisance of the role of the Internet and other ICT in the access and dissemination of information. All steps must be taken to ensure these new media's independence and ensure access of individuals to them (OHCHR 2011).

In 2016, the UN's Human Rights Council weighed in on whether internet access should be categorised as a fundamental right. In a non-binding resolution, the Promotion Protection and Enjoyment of Human Rights on the Internet, the Council underscores and affirms "the importance of applying a human rights-based approach in providing and in expanding access to Internet".[14] Understanding that Internet access transcends mere network connection, the Council advocates a holistic approach to eradicating digital poverty. Furthermore, the Council calls for bridging gender and disability initiated digital divides. Realising the relationship between the Internet and the actualisation of other human rights, it emphasises "the importance of building confidence and trust in the Internet," which has always been a barrier to using the Internet for development, innovation, cooperation, and education (Petri 2017). Although there is no explicit reference to access in the rural and insular areas, the specific mention of persons who have traditionally faced barriers to enjoying the full benefits of modern society makes this explicit.

At the regional level, the Council of Europe Conference of Ministers Responsible for Media and New Communication Services observed that with the strong reliance on Internet as a tool for everyday activities, there is an expectation that Internet services will be accessible and affordable, secure, reliable and ongoing.[15] Like the Human Rights Council, the Member States of the Council of Europe are to ensure that their national policy provides for universal internet access.[16] In 2016, the Committee of Ministers to member States on Internet freedom recommended that (i) internet access must be accessible and affordable without any discrimination; (ii) the public has access to the Internet in facilities supported by public administration (Internet access points), educational institutions or private owners (universal community service) and (iii) the provision of the Internet must be extended to those with low income, in rural or geographically remote areas and those with special needs (Council of Europe 2016).[17] Disappointedly, the document is a mere recommendation without any force law, and members could not be compelled to adopt it.

On the African Continent, while recognising the role of the Internet as a driving force in accelerating progress towards development in its various forms", the African Commission on Human and People's Rights (ACHPR) in 2016 issued a resolution on the Right to Freedom of Information and Expression on the Internet in Africa. The resolution calls on the African States to implement legislative and other measures to guarantee, respect and protect citizens' right to freedom of information and expression through access to Internet services (ACHPR 2016).[18] This resolution builds on the ACHPR objective advocating the right to freedom of information and expression as enshrined under Article 9 of the African Charter and other international human rights instruments. In a broader context, this is important if those rights protected offline are to enjoy protection online. Also, a Pan-African initiative, the African Declaration on Internet Rights and Freedoms was intended "to promote human rights standards and principles of openness in internet policy formulation and implementation on the continent." (African Declaration 2014).[19] Its Declaration states that "Access and affordability policies and regulations that foster universal and equal access to the Internet, including fair and transparent market regulation, universal service requirements and licensing agreements, must be adopted." (African Declaration 2014)[20] The declaration further notes that marginalised groups do not have equal access to the Internet, and special measures must be deployed to guarantee and preserve all rights exercisable online without discrimination. Disappointedly, the African Declaration is a soft law and merely advisory. No other African initiated instrument mandates the African government to provide internet access.

Part IV online learning beyond COVID19: the African perspective

There has been significant progress on internet access in Africa. The current internet penetration landscape had changed from what it was in 2000 when the whole continent had less Internet bandwidth than Luxembourg (ITU 2000). However, as of 2013, only 13% of all Africans used the Internet, compared to 36% globally, and more than half of urban African adults owned Internet-capable devices (McKinsey Global Institute 2013). By 2019, Internet penetration averaged 39.6% in Africa compared to 62.7% in the rest of the world (World Bank 2019). Comparably, Africa is very far from achieving the potential of the digital economy to benefit its population. There remains immense variation among African countries, ranging from 89.8% in Kenya to 5.3% in Burundi. Although many African governments have realised that connectivity is essential for economic development, there is no clear-cut African initiated treaty on internet provisions. Instead, this gap has been filled by regional arrangements and agency-led initiatives.

As argued above, Art 19 does not explicitly proclaim internet access a human right. Instead, La Rue opines that it could provide a right-based approach to internet access. The (Human Rights Council 2016) calls "all States to consider formulating … and adopting national Internet-related public policies that have the objective of universal access and enjoyment of human rights at their core."[21] Among the policies contemplated are "universal service" and "universal access". However, these policies are not construed as a fundamental right. Instead, they are enforceable right; some countries make provisions for them in their secondary legislation. This paper will now evaluate the implementation of universal service and universal access polices in Africa.

Universal service and universal access to the internet

Broadly, the terms "universal service" and "universal access" are used in different contexts to indicate government aspirations and policy objectives in guaranteeing that citizens participate in the benefits of modern economic life (Maddens 2009). They are policy aspirations designed to achieve equality and fairness of opportunity along with economic growth. Early discussions have always situated these policies in the context of telecommunication services, precisely, telephony. The evolving technological landscape has broadened this to include the availability of broadband networks, their adoption and use.[22]

Although "universal service" and "universal access" have been used synonymously, the two are distinct (González and Milne 2008). Universal service presupposes service for every household or individual (Xavier 2008). It guarantees " … those whose financial resources or geographical location do not allow them to access the basic services that are already available to and used by the great majority of citizens and which are considered essential for participation in society."[23] Universal access, on the other hand, contemplates public availability of services through means like payphones, community centres, public library and other public places. Central to both concepts is the three principles of availability, affordability and accessibility (Oestmann and Dymond 2008). In other words, the underlying objective of these policies is equal opportunities for uneconomic consumers and unprofitable areas that would have been excluded in the absence of such policy. For convenience, this paper will adopt the phraseology "Universal Access and Services" (UAS).

Various methods have been deployed in achieving UAS. Among them are: exclusivity periods for incumbent service providers, market reform, mandatory universal service obligations, regional or sub-regional licences and universal service funds. It also requires national governments to set up Universal Access Funds/Universal Service Funds to expand access.

Considering that UAS is a matter of economics, politics and social values, the debate on the elevation of internet access as a human right would be meaningless without a policy objective in support. Scholars have argued that "by preparing the foundation of an inclusive internet policy, African countries will increase their chances of integrating their citizens into digitised society, which eventually will have positive effects for social and economic development." (Wentrup et al. 2016). Adopting an appropriate policy is crucial in ensuring that those digitally disadvantaged can access the Internet. Such an approach must elevate UAS obligation above a sheer corporate social responsibility activity which is subject to the goodwill and generosity of investors and service providers. Significantly, UAS must be enshrined in national legislation, regulations and government policy documents. This will confer credibility, authority and enforceability on the policy and, more importantly, assist when evaluating its implementation and success.

Most African countries have included universal service policies in their overarching digital strategies. As of 2013, the International Telecommunication Union recorded that not less than thirty-one African countries have an existing UAS policy (ITU 2013). In West Africa, the Economic Community of West African States initiated a harmonisation process of UAS policies in the region. The ECOWAS Supplementary Act on Universal Access/Service was adopted in 2007.[24] The Act addresses six major issues: the creation of an appropriate regulatory and policy environment that fosters universal access/service; measures that can be taken to develop a national policy with realistic universal access/service objectives; role to be played by national regulators, policymakers and operators; telecommunications services to be included in universal service obligations; funding mechanisms; and cooperation in the area of universal access/service.[25] Despite this, the scope and definitions of UAS vary as many Member States have not maximised the Act.

Nonetheless, Ghana, Nigeria, and Senegal are leading countries in the region with well-established universal access strategies. For example, the Digital Senegal 2016–2025 Strategy calls for making broadband a priority through public-private partnerships for infrastructure sharing and deploying networks in unserved areas.[26] In addition, the strategy calls for the application of broadband across different regions, such as connecting schools, putting government services online and wider use of electronic commerce. The overall objective of the Senegalese strategy could be deduced from the slogan "the digital for all and for all uses in 2025 in Senegal with a dynamic and innovative private sector in an efficient ecosystem".[27] In Ghana, building on the Electronic Communications Act of 2008, the Ghanaian Broadband Strategy 2012 sets out the direction for Ghana's high-speed Internet. It, therefore, redefines universal service obligation for communication service providers to include *functional internet connection*. Furthermore, the strategy underscores the need to break the urban syndrome for broadband adoption favouring universal adoption to boost broadband access in rural areas.[28] Commendably, this strategy clarifies the definitional uncertainty on the distinction between universal access and universal service under the Electronic Communications Act of 2008. Whereas the legislation has confined universal service to telephony, making it appear that universal access is only applicable to broadband provision.

The silo approach to UAS among East African Community (EAC) the Member States led to disparate policies (Nyaga, Valcke, and Dumortier 2013). The EAC Model ICT Policy Framework aims to establish a harmonised system for regulating ICT services and networks in the region. While noting the problem of limited and poor rural connectivity, affordability and availability of ICTs in underserved areas, and lack of knowledge-sharing networks at the grassroots level, the framework mandates Members States to establish UAS Fund for the ICT sector to meet UAS objectives.[29] Disappointedly, this policy framework is very rudimentary and not far-reaching.[30] Many key terms are left undefined while the development of the Framework remain demitted for the Member States and National Regulatory Authorities (NRAs). Moreover, unlike the ECOWAS UAS framework primarily devoted to universal access, the EAC framework ambition to cover many issues resulted in a superficial treatment of internet access.

All EAC countries, except South Sudan, currently have some form of national broadband policy or strategy. Uganda is ahead of other big EAC Member States like Kenya and Tanzania. The 2005 Communications (Universal Service) Regulations provides a comprehensive universal policy service for Uganda. It adopts a broad definition of universal service obligation.[31] The regulation mandates the Uganda Communications Commission (UCC) to support the provision of universal service obligations by the operators. One main objective of UCC is to promote widespread access to quality services at affordable rates and ensure that rural and high-cost areas have access to communication and information services at prices reasonably comparable with those offered in urban areas.[32] The Information and Communications (Universal Access and Service) Regulations 2010 contains the Kenyan approach to internet access. Unlike the Ugandan Regulation, the Kenyan regulation bifurcates universal access and universal service from a private-public perspective. It, however, shares a similar objective in providing access by promoting the building of communications infrastructure and services rollout in rural, remote and under-served areas.

Arguably, s32 of the South African provides a constitutional basis for access to the Internet as a form of human right under the right of access to information. The South African court reasoned that "[a]ccess to information and the facilitation of learning and understanding *are essential for meaningful involvement* of ordinary citizens in public life. This ... reflects the foundational principle of democratic government which ensures accountability, responsiveness and openness."[33] The s32 provision is amplified by two principal government ICT policies: (i) South Africa Connect: Creating Opportunities, Ensuring Inclusion (South Africa's Broadband Policy),[34] and (ii) the National Integrated ICT Policy White Paper (DPTS 2016)[35] The latter emphasises the interplay between access to the Internet and the constitutional right to equality. The White Paper contains the overarching policy framework in transforming South Africa into an inclusive and innovative digital society. Chapter 5 deals with UAS. It identifies two priority areas, namely: (i) Increasing coverage to rural, remote and underserviced areas, and (ii) Digital inclusion of all segments of society, with priority being given to support persons with disabilities, persons with limited or no income, and public institutions fulfilling specific public needs (such as schools, clinics and hospitals, and police stations).

In addition to the policy papers, the South African government have enacted other legislation that implicates access to online information: the Promotion of Access to Information Act 2000 and the Electronic Communications and Transactions Act 2002 (ECTA) and Electronic Communication Act 2005 (ECA). The ECTA universal service mandate is very instructive. The Act requires that the national e-strategy provide connectivity to disadvantaged communities; encourage the private sector to initiate schemes to universal access; foster the adoption and use of new technologies for attaining universal access; stimulate public awareness, understanding and acceptance of benefits of internet connectivity and electronic transacting.[36]

Apparently, the problem with Africa internet access is not the absence of UAS policy or legislation. Instead, the hurdle is the effective implementation and policy mismatch. For instance, commercial mobile phone penetration has been pursued to the detriment of broadband access. (Dorward 2013) argues that poorly designed legal and policy frameworks hinder the ability of USF to be transformative in terms of widening its scope to reflect technological and service changes. Besides, there has been a stark failure in the enforcement of Universal Service Obligation. First, there is poor or no utilisation of universal service funds (USF). USF is established to ameliorate the failure of the market to cater for the wider societal need (Msimang 2012). For example, the Egyptian policy document says that the purpose of its USF is to provide affordable basic telecommunications services for all citizens, particularly those in 'economically non-feasible regions of the country.[37] On the other hand, the Tanzanian USF aims to ensure the availability of 'communication services' in the disadvantaged area to promote socio-economic development.[38] Thus, USFs are designed to compensate service providers for extending their services to underserved and disadvantaged areas.[39] Despite the USFs role in furthering access, the disbursement has been very slow or inactive even where funds are continued to be generated. Disappointedly, the Ivorian government waited for eight years before disbursing its funds, while DR Congo is yet to begin the disbursement of its fund. Of the 23 USFs surveyed in sub-Saharan Africa, more than a third is yet to disburse or partial disbursement. In 2018, an estimated USD 408 million sat un-distributed in USFs across 37 African countries (Thakur and Potter 2018). These low fund activity levels are the product of regulatory bottleneck, lack of political will and lack of technical know.

Second, the underlying regulatory framework for UAS and its funding through USFs is faulty. Whereas enabling legal and regulatory framework for UAS must be robust, flexible and technologically neutral. However, the UAS policies of many African countries are stuck in the provision of universal service to fixed telephone lines as opposed to internet access. Expectedly, the definitions of UAS are narrowly couched and exclude dial-up internet, wireless and broadband services. This provides an understanding of the failure and catastrophic experience that underline learning during COVID19. Only ten of twenty-three countries included in a report permits their USFs to be spent on the provision of wireless internet service while only six countries make provisions for broadband services. Countries like Cameron, Gabon, Mali, Mauritania, and Niger fail to invest in infrastructure. The review process of changing the focus of USF is either too slow or not happening at all; hence, idle funds cannot be disbursed for emerging technology like broadband as this was not their original mandate (Dorward 2013).

Third, a related issue to the enforcement of the UAS obligation is its justiciability. If internet access is classified as a human right, further clarification is needed as to its nature. Although internet access intersects with civil and political rights, arguably, it will fall under social and economic rights. However, at the domestic level, there are doubts about the enforcement of social and economic rights (Yeshanew 2013). It is unclear whether courts can legitimately adjudicate economic and social issues. However, Yeshanew 2013 argues that the protection of socio-economic, cultural rights as substantive norms and their subjection to adjudicatory enforcement by the African Commission means that the rights are generally justiciable (Yeshanew 2011). Only South Africa provides a constitutional basis for access to the Internet but as a corollary right under the right of access to information. Socio-economic rights are clearly justiciable under South African law,[40] but they are not in many other African countries.[41] For instance, in a country like Nigeria, socio-economic rights listed under the Chapter II of the Nigerian Constitution are not regarded as enforceable.[42] In Uganda, the Constitutional court in *CEHURD & Others v Attorney General of Uganda* underscored the difficulty of enforcing a socio-economic right, in this case, the right to health.[43] In countries where these rights are enforceable, they remain limited by litigation costs, limited access to court and complicated legal structure(Gloppen and Kanyongolo 2007).

Policy and regulation initiative for digital Africa (PRIDA)

Digital transformation requires the introduction of appropriate policy and regulation. Without this, policymakers are left applying 'analogue' approaches to entirely new problems. Scholars have underscored the importance of new analytical frameworks and decision tools if any continent desires to transition from an analogue into the future of the globalised digital economy (Zanatta and Kira 2018). In 2017, a collaboration, the Policy and Regulation Initiative for Digital Africa (PRIDA) was initiated among others to evaluate harmonise measurable ICT/Telecommunications policy, legal and regulatory framework.

PRIDA is a joint initiative of the African Union (AU), the European Union (EU) and the International Telecommunication Union (ITU). It is a three-year initiative (2018 - 2022) supported by the EU-funded Pan African Programme. Regulatory uncertainty and policy gaps discourage investment in the ICT sector resulting in unaffordable broadband prices. PRIDA aims to foster universally accessible and affordable broadband across the continent to unlock future benefits of internet-based services.[44] Its overall objective is to create a more harmonised and enabling regulatory framework for the use of Information and Communication Technology for social and economic development, with an emphasis on boosting the spectrum market across Africa.[45]

Considering that Internet access in Africa has been hindered by inefficient regulatory environments, lack of coherent regional infrastructure policies, and political interference. It is hoped that PRIDA digital platform will serve as a continental virtual space that provides one space for all national, regional and continental related ICT policies, legislations and Regulations. It will be the tool to support harmonisation of these policies and regulations and a mechanism to collect ICT & Internet data from undertaking statistics to monitor and evaluate the progress to truly reflect African countries realities with regard to broadband penetration and preparedness to digitalisation. It should be noted that an efficient regulatory environment and harmonised policies have the tendency to build a consolidated continental digital ecosystem, address the root causes of market failure in Africa, foster the development of an inclusive digital economy and contribute to consumer welfare. Besides, it will increase competition and widen entry into ICT markets across the continent for more efficiency and affordability of services.

The digital transformation strategy for Africa

Working with the UN Economic Commission for Africa, Smart Africa, AUDA-NEPAD, Regional Economic Communities, African Development Bank, Africa Telecommunications Union, Africa Capacity Building Foundation, International Telecommunication Union and the World Bank, the African Union Commission prepared a comprehensive Digital Transformation Strategy for Africa.[46] The strategy was endorsed by the Thirty–Sixth Ordinary Session of the African Union Executive Council held in February 2020. The DTS envisions an.

> "integrated and inclusive digital society and economy in Africa that improves the quality of life of Africa's citizens, strengthen[s] the existing economic sector, enable[s] its diversification and development, and ensure[s] continental ownership with Africa as a producer and not only a consumer in the global economy". (African Union 2020)[47]

The DTS builds on existing initiatives and frameworks, such as the Policy and Regulatory Initiative for Digital Africa (PRIDA), the Programme for Infrastructure Development in Africa (PRIDA), the African Continental Free Trade Area (AfCFTA), the African Union Financial Institutions (AUFIs, the Single African Air Transport Market (SAATM); and the Free Movement of Persons (FMP) to support the development of a Digital Single Market (DSM) for Africa, as part of the integration priorities of the African Union. The DTS sets its overall objective as follows: "to harness digital technologies and innovation to transform African societies and economies to promote Africa's integration, generate inclusive economic growth, stimulate job creation, break the digital divide, and eradicate poverty for the continent's socio-economic development and ensure Africa's ownership of modern tools of digital management."[48]

One of the problems identified in this paper is the absence of appropriate policies that support internet access in some African countries, especially investment in rural and remote areas. The DTS contains the following specific objectives:

- Create a harmonised environment necessary to guarantee investment and financing by setting up a digital sovereignty fund in order to close the digital infrastructure gap and achieve an accessible, affordable and secure broadband, across demography, gender, and geography;
- Harmonise policies, legislations and regulations and establish and improve digital networks and services with a view to strengthening intra-Africa trade, intra-investment and capital flows and the socio-economic integration of the continent, while maintaining a relational balance with other continents in the context of networked economies (Digital economy, collaborative economy)
- Implement laws, policies and regulations required to stimulate and accelerate digital transformation for national, regional and continental development;[49]

Part VII (A) of DTS requires governments to create an enabling environment with policies and regulations that promote digital transformation. Policy, legal and regulatory framework must be flexible, up-to-date, incentive-based and market driven if they are to promote digital transformation. Policy stability and predictability motivate investors to innovate and take business risks. It recommends that policy design must take holistic approach be human-centred. Specifically, "Special attention should be given to women, people living in remote areas, people with disabilities, disadvantaged and marginalised communities through the establishment of a platform for dialogue and social cohesion and dialogue that involves these groups targets. The promotion of online cultural diversity must be supported to ensure that every person participates fully in society." While it is hoped that the implementation will address the policy failure of UAS, it does not address whether legal and regulatory framework should consider classifying the right to Internet as human right.

Of specific relevance to internet penetration and broadband availability is Part VII B which addresses provision of digital infrastructure. DTS recognises the role of affordable, accessible and reliable infrastructure in achieving inclusive digital access. However, because internet penetration is mobile phone driven, unmetered pricing is not common in Africa. The DTS seeks governments to promote measures that increase the affordability of broadband and technology devices & services. For example, governments or their relevant agencies must maximise Universal Service Funds in extending infrastructure to underserved areas and reduce access pricing; adopt appropriate policy and regulation in areas such as taxation to promote the affordability of Internet; prioritise connections to public buildings such as libraries and schools; and ensure access to affordable devices to people living with disability, elderly and the disadvantaged to access the Internet.

On the relationship between internet access and education, there is an admission that the continent has failed to introduce technology in education. This is due to reasons not limited to technical barriers, policy and regulatory constraints, and capacity to manage the integration of technology in education. In rectifying the disjunction between education and internet access, the DTS adopts a holistic approach by advocating that ICT should be introduced to all levels of education and both formal and informal. It identifies that:

> Connecting Africa's universities, skills-training institutions and secondary schools with broadband Internet is essential if the continent is to realise the potential of digital technologies in education. Further, all young people need to acquire digital skills at the basic and intermediate levels if they are to use technology. Integration of digital skills training into the core curriculum of formal education courses for all learners, irrespective of their specialisation, is essential.[50]

Considering that education has become another form of export, connecting African schools with broadband is imperative if the continent's educational sector is to be competitive in post COVID19 era. In addition, African research institutions need to be connected to a stable internet grid for the purpose of collaboration, grants applications and ground-breaking research. Beyond this, investment in broadband drives economic growth, productivity and innovation.

Conclusion

The dynamics of internet access range from political, economic, to social. Its intersection with other rights and integration into quotidian activities provide ample justifications for its elevation to a human rights status. The consequence of the lack of such status was felt in both developed and developing countries alike during the COVID19 lockdown.

Though there are commendable developments in internet penetration in Africa, the continent still lags compared to other regions of the world. Mobile internet penetration gives false positives on Africa's internet landscape. Internet access remains expensive, and the connection is unreliable. The experience during the COVID19 shutdown in 2020 underlines that most countries in Africa have not effectively integrated the Internet into the learning process. And the victims of this failure are not just the pupils but includes their parents and educational establishments. Lack of political will, outdated policies and non-implementation of UAS objectives are among the many factors that still make Africa remains a digital desert. With the experience of COVID19 relatively behind, this article hopes that the emerging digital strategies in Africa could be utilised in enhancing access to the Internet and its integration into learning.

Notes

1. See https://www.un.org/sustainabledevelopment/infrastructure-industrialization/ Goal 9

2. Ibid 33 of the 47 Least Developed Countries are on the African Continent.
3. For example, on the 15 March 2020, the Ghanaian government banned all public gatherings including conferences, workshops, funerals, festivals, political rallies, church activities and other related events at a press briefing on the state of COVID-19 while the South African government announced a 2-day lockdown on the 23 March 2020.
4. For examples of tuition being charged by private schools in South Africa, please see https://businesstech.co.za/news/trending/459994/the-most-expensive-schools-in-south-africa-in-2021/
5. https://www.globalpartnership.org/where-we-work/cote-divoire
6. For examples on responses of African countries to learning during COVID19, please see National learning platforms and tools https://en.unesco.org/covid19/educationresponse/nationalresponses
7. International Energy Agency *Africa Energy Outlook 2019*
8. https://en.unesco.org/news/learning-through-radio-and-television-time-covid-19
9. Loon is a network of stratospheric balloons that provide internet connectivity to rural and remote communities. "The high-altitude balloons in the stratosphere create an aerial wireless network with up to 4G-LTE speeds. Users connect to the balloon network using a special Internet antenna attached to their building." A single balloon can provide internet connectivity across an 80km diameter area.
10. [2020] eKLR available http://kenyalaw.org/caselaw/cases/view/199128/
11. Ibid [46]
12. Ibid
13. Human Rights Council Thirty-second session Agenda item 3 Promotion and protection of all human rights, civil, political, economic, social and cultural rights, including the right to development [D]ecides to continue its consideration of the promotion, protection and enjoyment of human rights, including the right to freedom of expression, on the Internet and other information and communication technology, as well as of how the Internet can be an important tool for fostering citizen and civil society participation, for the realization of development in every community and for exercising human rights, in accordance with its programme of work
14. http://ap.ohchr.org/documents/E/HRC/d_res_dec/A_HRC_32_L20.docx
15. First Council of Europe Conference of Ministers Responsible for Media and New Communication Services (Reykjavik, Iceland, May 29, 2009), MCM (2009) 011, Political Declaration, para.5.
16. See Council of Europe and Internet Freedom: From Principles to Global Treaty Law
17. Recommendation CM/Rec(2016)5 of the Committee of Ministers to member States on Internet freedom (Adopted by the Committee of Ministers on 13 April 2016 at the 1253rd meeting of the Ministers' Deputies)available at https://search.coe.int/cm/Pages/result_details.aspx?ObjectId=09000016806415fa
18. 362 Resolution on the Right to Freedom of Information and Expression on the Internet in Africa - ACHPR/Res.362(LIX)2016
19. See the African Declaration on Internet Rights and Freedoms 2014 https://africaninternetrights.org/en/about
20. See the African Declaration on Internet Rights and Freedoms 2014 https://africaninternetrights.org/sites/default/files/African-Declaration-English-FINAL.pdf
21. See Human Right Council 32 Session on the the Promotion, protection and enjoyment of human rights on the Internet http://ap.ohchr.org/documents/E/HRC/d_res_dec/A_HRC_32_L20.docx
22. For example, the US Communications Act 1996 was introduced to pave way for the recognition of the Internet as new ICT
23. See the Communication from the Commission to the Council, the European Parliament, the European Economic and Social committee and the Committee of the Regions On the Review of the Scope of Universal Service in accordance with Article 15 of Directive 2002/22/EC [SEC (2005)660] /* COM/2005/0203 final */
24. See ECOWAS Supplementary Act A/SA.601/07

25. See Ibid Art 3
26. ITU 2018 *Measuring the Information Society Report Volume 2. ICT Country Profiles* available at https://www.itu.int/en/ITU-D/Statistics/Documents/publications/misr2018/MISR-2018-Vol-2-E.pdf
27. See IST Africa "Introduction: Republic of Senegal" https://www.ist-africa.org/home/default.asp?page=doc-by-id&docid=5558
28. Ibid
29. See East African Communication Organisation ICT POLICY & REGULATORY FRAMEWORK HARMONIZATION http://www.eaco.int/admin/docs/reports/Draft_Model_ICT_Policy_KGJ_March_2015.pdf
30. EACO EAC MODEL ICT REGULATORY FRAMEWORK 2017 http://www.eaco.int/admin/docs/publications/EAC%20MODEL%20ICT%20REGULATORY%20FRAMEWORK.pdf
31. The 2005 Communications (Universal Service) Regulations s5
32. S3(e)
33. See the case of *South African Broadcasting Corporation v Director of Public Prosecution* (CCT58/06) [2006] ZACC 15 para 28 emphasis supplied
34. Department of Communications. (2013). South Africa Connect: Creating Opportunities, Ensuring Inclusion (South Africa's Broadband Policy). www.gov.za/documents/electronic- communications-act-south-africaconnect-creating-opportunity-ensuring-inclusion
35. Hereinafter the White Paper
36. ECTA s6
37. Universal Service Fund Policy (Final) (2017), Egypt.
38. UCSAF 2014. The Ghana Investment Fund for Electronic Communications (GIFEC) aims to provide financial resources for the establishment of universal service and ensure access to ICT and basic telephony, by rural communities in Ghana. This includes facilitating and providing internet, multimedia, broadband service to unserved and underserved rural communities. See Patrick Ohemeng Gyaase, Augustine Takyi "A Case for Public Financing of Broadband Internet Infrastructure In Ghana" (2014) 3(2) International Journal of Scientific & Technology Research 60–68
39. To correct the imbalance therefore the government, through the Ghana Investment Fund for Electronic Communications (GIFEC), has also initiated projects that will facilitate citizens' access to connectivity and thereby government activities. They include the school connectivity program, which aims to install internet access and computers and other IT accessories in all senior secondary schools and colleges of teacher education, as well as technical and vocational schools.
40. *Republic of South Africa v. Grootboom 2000 (11) BCLR 1169 (CC) (S. Afr.).*
41. On justiciability in Malawi, see *Ministry of Finance ex-parte SGS Malawi Limited Miscellaneous Civil Cause Number 40 of 2003.*
42. Nigerian Constitution 1999 as amended s6(6)c; See also Archbishop Anthony Okogie v. AG Lagos State (1981) 2 NCLR 337 at 350
43. Constitutional Petition No. 16 of 2011
44. https://africa-eu-partnership.org/en/projects/policy-and-regulation-initiative-digital-africa-prida
45. PRIDA "Policy Harmonisation" available at https://oneprida.africa/policy-harmonisation/
46. African Union "The Digital Transformation Strategy for Africa (2020-2030)" https://au.int/en/documents/20200518/digital-transformation-strategy-africa-2020-2030
47. Ibid
48. Ibid
49. Ibid
50. Ibid

Disclosure statement

No potential conflict of interest was reported by the author(s).

References

Communication from the Commission to the Council, the European Parliament, the European Economic and Social committee and the Committee of the Regions On the Review of the Scope of Universal Service in accordance with Article 15 of Directive 2002/22/EC [SEC (2005)660] /* COM/2005/0203 final */.

ACAPS. 2020. "Education & child protection challenges in Eastern DRC: Impact of COVID-19, conflict and policy reform" available at https://reliefweb.int/sites/reliefweb.int/files/resources/20201019_acaps_covid-19_thematic_series_on_education_drc_eastern_provinces.pdf.

Adewuyi, O. B., M. K. Kiptoo, A. F. Afolayan, T. Amara, O. I. Alawode, and T. Senjyu. 2000. "Challenges and Prospects of Nigeria's Sustainable Energy Transition with Lessons from Other Countries' Experiences." *Energy Reports* 6: 993–1009. doi:10.1016/j.egyr.2020.04.022.

African Declaration on Internet Rights and Freedoms. 2014. Available at https://africaninternetrights.org/en/about`

African Commission on Human and Peoples' Rights (ACPHR). 2016. "362 Resolution on the Right to Freedom of Information and Expression on the Internet in Africa" - ACHPR/Res.362(LIX) 2016.

African Union. 2020. "The Digital Transformation Strategy for Africa (2020–2030)" https://au.int/en/documents/20200518/digital-transformation-strategy-africa-2020-2030.

Association for the Development of Education in Africa. 2020. "Impact of COVID19 on Africa's Education: Reflecting on Promising Interventions and Challenges, towards a New Normal" Final Report August 2020 available at https://www.adeanet.org/sites/default/files/impact_of_covid-19_on_africas_education_final_report.pdf.

Association for the Development of Education in Africa (ADEA). 2020. "COVID19 Impact on Education in African Countries" available at https://www.adeanet.org/sites/default/files/report_summary_covid-19_impact.pdf.

Bigaba, Elie. 2020. "Coronavirus en RDC: Félix Tshisekedi annonce la fermeture des écoles, Universités et Églises à partir de ce jeudi" 19 Mars avaiable at https://jambordc.info/17030/.

Brew-Hammond, Abeeku, and Francis Kemausuor. 2009. "Energy for all in Africa — to be or not to be?!." *Current Opinion in Environmental Sustainability 2009* 1: 83–88. doi:10.1016/j.cosust.2009.07.014.

Castells, M. 2010. *End of Millennium*. 2nd ed. Oxford: Blackwell.

Coccoli, J. 2017. "The Challenges of New Technologies in the Implementation of Human Rights: An Analysis of Some Critical Issues in the Digital Era." *Peace Human Rights Governance* 1 (2): 223–250.

Coleman, V. 2021. *Digital Divide in UK Education During COVID-19 Pandemic: Literature Review. Cambridge Assessment Research Report*. Cambridge, UK: Cambridge Assessment.

Council of Europe Recommendation CM/Rec. 2016. 5 of the Committee of Ministers to member States on Internet freedom *(Adopted by the Committee of Ministers on 13 April 2016 at the 1253rd meeting of the Ministers' Deputies)available at* https://search.coe.int/cm/Pages/result_details.aspx?ObjectId=09000016806415fa.

Davids, N. 2020. "Maybe the coronavirus will set SA on a path to a more equitable education system" News24. Available at https://m.news24.com/Columnists/GuestColumn/opinion-maybe-the-coronavirus-will-set-south-africa-on-the-path-to-a-more-equitable-education-system-20200327.

Department of Communications. 2013. South Africa Connect: Creating Opportunities, Ensuring Inclusion (South Africa's Broadband Policy). www.gov.za/documents/electronic-communications-act-south-africaconnect-creating-opportunity-ensuring-inclusion.

Dorward, L. A. 2013. *Regulatory and Market Environment: Universal Service Fund and Digital Inclusion for All*.

DTPS. 2016. National Integrated ICT Policy White Paper. https://www.dtps.gov.za/images/phocagallery/Popular_Topic_Pictures/National_Integrated_ICT_Policy_White.pdf.

du Toit, Jean, and Anné H. Verhoef. 2018. "Embodied Digital Technology and Transformation in Higher Education." *Transformation in Higher Education [Online]* 3.

Dzair Daily. Available at https://www.dzairdaily.com/cours-en-ligne-algerie-liste-chaine-scolaireyoutube-bac-bem-2020/.

EACO EAC MODEL ICT REGULATORY FRAMEWORK. 2017. http://www.eaco.int/admin/docs/publications/EAC%20MODEL%20ICT%20REGULATORY%20FRAMEWORK.pdf.

East African Communication Organisation. 2015. "ICT Policy & Regulatory Framework Harmonization" http://www.eaco.int/admin/docs/reports/Draft_Model_ICT_Policy_KGJ_March_2015.pdf.

Edo, S., H. Okodua, and J. Odebiyi. 2019. "Internet Adoption and Financial Development in Sub-Saharan Africa: Evidence from Nigeria and Kenya." *African Development Review* 31 (1): 144–160. doi:10.1111/1467-8268.12370.

EdTech Hub. 2020. "The Effect of COVID-19 on Education in Africa and its implications for the Use of Technology: A survey of the Experience and Opinions of Educators and Technology Specialists UKAid September 2020.

European Training Foundation. 2020. "Algeria: Distance Learning for Students" available at https://www.etf.europa.eu/en/news-and-events/news/algeria-distance-learning-students.

Faturoti, B. 2021. "The CJEU and the Educational Exception in Renckhoff: Permitted to View but not to Share." In *The Future of Intellectual Property*, edited by D. Gervais, 229. Edward Elgar 2021.

Feenberg, A. 1991. *Critical Theory of Technology*. Oxford: Oxford University Press. 5.

Gloppen, S., and F. E. Kanyongolo. 2007. "Courts and the Poor in Malawi: Economic Marginalization, Vulnerability and the Law." *International Journal of Constitutional Law* 5: 258–93. doi:10.1093/icon/mom002.

González, C. F., and C. Milne. 2008. "Re-thinking Universal Service Policy for the Digital Era: Setting the Scene." *INFO* 10 (5–6): 4–11. JRC46885

GSMA. 2015. "Digital inclusion and mobile sector taxation in the Democratic Republic of the Congo" Nov 2015.

Gunkel, David J. 2020. "Perspectives on Ethics of AI: Philosophy." In edited by Markus D. Dubber, Frank Pasquale, and Sunit Das. The Oxford Handbook of Ethics of AI Oxford University Press.

Gyaase, P. O., and Augustine Takyi. 2014. "A Case for Public Financing of Broadband Internet Infrastructure In Ghana." *International Journal of Scientific & Technology Research* 3 (2): 60–68.

Hadjeris, F. 2021 . "Revisiting Sustainable Development Goal 4 in the Context of COVID-19 Pandemic: A Case Study of Online Teaching in Algerian Higher Education Institutions." *Hum Behav & Emerg Tech* 3: 160–168. doi:10.1002/hbe2.245.

Hodges, C., S. Moore, B. Lockee, T. Trust, and M. Bond. 2020. "The Difference between Emergency Remote Teaching and Online Learning. Available at: https://er.educause.edu/articles/2020/3/the-difference-between-emergency-remote-teaching-and-online-learning.

Human Rights Watch. 2020. "Impact of COVID19 On Children's Education in Africa: Submission to the African Committee of Experts on the Rights and Welfare of the Child" 35th Ordinary Session 31 August – 4 September.

Inman, E., M. Kerwin, and L. Mayes. 1999. "Instructor and Student Attitudes Toward Distance Learning." *Community College Journal of Research & Practice* 23 (6): 581–592. doi:10.1080/106689299264594.

International Energy Agency. 2019. *Africa Energy Outlook* 2019 available from https://www.iea.org/reports/africa-energy-outlook-2019.

ITU. 2000. Improving IP Connectivity in the Least Developed Countries. www.itu.int.

ITU. 2003. "World Summit on the Information Society Declaration Principles: Building the Information Society: a global challenge in the new Millennium Document" WSIS-03/GENEVA/DOC/4-E 12 December 2003 available at http://www.itu.int/net/wsis/docs/geneva/official/dop.html.

ITU. 2013. *Universal Service Fund and Digital Inclusion for all Study* 2013 https://www.itu.int/en/ITU-D/Digital-Inclusion/Pages/Digital_Inclusion_Resources/Universal_Service_Funds_Digital_Inclusion.aspx.

ITU. 2018. *Measuring the Information Society Report Volume 2. ICT Country Profiles* available at https://www.itu.int/en/ITU-D/Statistics/Documents/publications/misr2018/MISR-2018-Vol-2-E.pdf.

Jody, Nkashama. 2020. "Universities reopen despite ongoing spread of COVID-19" *World University News* 25 August 2020 https://www.universityworldnews.com/post.php?story=20200825111737663.

Johnson, J. 2021. "Share of internet users in Africa as of December 2020, by country" available at https://www.statista.com/statistics/1124283/internet-penetration-in-africa-by-country/.

LaRue, F. United Nations Human Rights Council. 2011, May 16. *Report of the Special Rapporteur on the Promotion and Protection of the Right to Freedom of Opinion and Expression, Frank La Rue*. Geneva: United Nations.

Le-Grange, L. 2004. "E-learning: Some Critical Thoughts." *South African Journal of Higher Education* 18 (1): 87–97. doi:10.4314/sajhe.v18i1.25430.

Le Grange, L. 2020. Covid-19 pandemic and the prospects of education in South Africa" *Prospects* Available doi:10.1007/s11125-020-09514-w

Maddens, S. 2009. "Trends in Universal Access and Service Policies: Changing Policies to Accommodate." *ITU Publishing*.

McKinsey Global Institute. 2013. "Lions go digital: The Internet's transformative potential in Africa" available at http://www.mckinsey.com/industries/high-tech/our-insights/lions-go-digital-the-internets-transformative-potential-in-africa.

Msimang, M. 2012. "The More Things Change, the More They Stay the Same: Strategies for Financing Universal Broadband Access." *in Trends Telecommunication Reform 2012 - Smart Regulation in a Broadband World (ITU 2012)*, 79–110.

Nkashama, Jody. August 2020. "Universities reopen despite ongoing spread of COVID-19" (University World News: Africa Edition). Available at https://www.universityworldnews.com/post.php?story=20200825111737663

Nyaga, J. K., Peggy Valcke, and Jos Dumortier. 2013. "Regulatory Convergence of ICT Sectors in the East African Community (EAC): Challenges for the Current Legislative and Regulatory Frameworks and Lessons from the European Union Experience." *2013 IST-AFRICA PROCEEDINGS* 1 (2013).

OECD. 2020. Strengthening online learning when schools are closed: The role of families and teachers in supporting students during the COVID-19 crisis available at https://www.oecd.org/coronavirus/policy-responses/strengthening-online-learning-when-schools-are-closed-the-role-of-families-and-teachers-in-supporting-students-during-the-covid-19-crisis-c4ecba6c/.

Oestmann, S., and A. Dymond. 2008. *Universal Access and Service: Module 4, ICT Toolkit*. Washington, DC. Retrieved from www.ictregulationtoolkit.org

OHCHR. 2011. International Covenant on Civil and Political Rights *General Comment* No. 34. *Article 19*: Freedoms of opinion and expression. http://ap.ohchr.org/documents/E/HRC/d_res_dec/A_HRC_32_L20.docx.

Oxford Business Group. 2018. "Reforms to Algeria's education system to expand capacity and modernise curricula / Algeria 2018 / Oxford Business Group," https://oxfordbusinessgroup.com/overview/contemporary-tutelage-transforming-education-system-expand-capacity-and-prepare-students-modern-age.

Parsitau, D. S., and E. Jepkemei. 2020. "How school closures during COVID-19 further marginalize vulnerable children in Kenya" *Education Plus Development Brookings Institution* available at https://www.brookings.edu/blog/education-plus-development/2020/05/06/how-school-closures-during-covid-19-further-marginalize-vulnerable-children-in-kenya/.

Petri, Claire. 2017. "Rural Libraries and the Human Right to Internet Access." In *Rural and Small Public Libraries: Challenges and Opportunities (Advances in Librarianship, Vol. 43)*, edited by B. Real, 13–35. Bingley: Emerald Publishing Limited.

PRIDA. "Policy Harmonisation" available at https://oneprida.africa/policy-harmonisation/.

Redouane, L. 2020. "Cours en ligne en Algérie: La liste des chaînes scolaires sur YouTube.".

Rens, Andrew. 2020. "The Right to Education and the Internet: Case Study on the Role of the Internet in Provision and Accessibility of Educational Resources in South Africa." *APC (May 2016)* 3.

South Africa Department of Communications. 2013. South Africa Connect: Creating Opportunities, Ensuring Inclusion (South Africa's Broadband Policy). Available at www.gov.za/documents/electronic-communications-act-south-africaconnect-creating-opportunity-ensuring-inclusion.

Soyemi, A. O., I. A. Samuel, A. Adesina, A. Akinmeji, and A. Favour. 2021. "A Robust Energy Policy Review of Selected African Countries: An Impetus for Energy Sustainability in Nigeria." *J. Phys.: Conf. Ser*, 1734.

Steele, C. 2019. "What is the Digital Divide? Digital Divide Council" Available at: http://www.digitaldividecouncil.com/what-is-the-digital-divide/.

Thakur, D., and L. Potter. 2018. *Universal Service and Access Funds: An Untapped Resource to Close the Gender Digital Divide*. Washington, DC: Web Foundation 2018.

Tully, S. 2006. "The Human Right to Access Electricity." *Electr J* 19 (3): 30–39. doi:10.1016/j.tej.2006.02.003.

UNESCO. 2020. "Learning through radio and television in the time of COVID-19" https://en.unesco.org/news/learning-through-radio-and-television-time-covid-19.

United Nations. 2020a. A/RES/55/2. General Assembly. Distr.: General. 18 September 2000. Available at https://www.un.org/en/development/desa/population/migration/generalassembly/docs/globalcompact/A_RES_55_2.pdf.

United Nations. 2020b. "Policy Brief: Education during COVID-19 and beyond" August 2020 available at https://www.un.org/development/desa/dspd/wp-content/uploads/sites/22/2020/08/sg_policy_brief_covid-19_and_education_august_2020.pdf.

Wentrup, Robert, Xiangxuan Xu, H. Richard Nakamura, and Patrik Ström. 2016. "Crossing the Digital Desert in Sub-Saharan Africa: Does Policy Matter." *Policy & Internet* 8 (3): 248–269. doi:10.1002/poi3.123.

Woessmann, Ludger, Vera Freundl, Elisabeth Grewenig, Philipp Lergetporer, Katharina Werner, and Larissa Zierow. 2020. "Bildung in der Corona-Krise: Wie Haben die Schulkinder die Zeit der Schulschließungen Verbracht, und Welche Bildungsmaßnahmen Befürworten die Deutschen?" *ifo Schnelldienst* 73 (9): 25–39.

World Bank. 2019. "Achieving Broadband Access for All in Africa Comes With a $100 Billion Price Tag" available at https://www.worldbank.org/en/news/press-release/2019/10/17/achieving-broadband-access-for-all-in-africa-comes-with-a-100-billion-price-tag.

Xavier, P. 2008. "From Universal Service to Universal Network Access." *info* 10 (5/6): 20–32. doi:10.1108/14636690810904689.

Yeshanew, S. A. 2011. "Approaches to the Justiciability of Economic, Social and Cultural Rights in the Jurisprudence of the African Commission on Human and Peoples' Rights: Progress and Perspectives." *African Human Rights Law Journal* 11: 317.

Yeshanew, S. A. 2013. *The Justiciability of Economic, Social and Cultural Rights in the African Regional Human Rights System: Theory, Practice and Prospect*. Intersentia.

Yorke, L., P. Rose, B. Hagos, and T. Woldehanna. 2020. The effects of COVID-19 on primary education in Ethiopia: Perspectives of school principals and teachers" Research and Policy Paper No. 20/10. REAL Centre, University of Cambridge.

Zanatta, R. A., and B. Kira. 2018. "Regulation of Uber in São Paulo: From Conflict to Regulatory Experimentation." *International Journal of Private Law* 9 (1–2): 83–94. doi:10.1504/IJPL.2018.097332.

Zermane, H., and S. Aitouche. 2020. "Digital Learning With COVID-19 in Algeria." *International Journal of 3D Printing Technologies and Digital Industry* 4 (2): 161–170. doi:10.46519/ij3dptdi.776978.

Index

Note: **Bold** page numbers refer to tables and page numbers followed by "n" denote endnotes.

FSC
www.fsc.org
MIX
Papier | Fördert gute Waldnutzung
FSC® C083411

Kolibri 360 GmbH
Ferdinand-Jühlke-Straße 7
99095 Erfurt, Deutschland
produktsicherheit@kolibri360.de